ARE YOU PRAYING FOR THE WRONG THING?

ARE YOU PRAYING FOR THE WRONG THING?

LEARNING TO ASK WHAT GOD WANTS FOR YOU, NOT JUST WHAT YOU WANT

TRAVIS GREENE

NELSON
BOOKS

An Imprint of Thomas Nelson

Published in Nashville, Tennessee, by Nelson Books, an imprint of Thomas Nelson. Nelson Books and Thomas Nelson are registered trademarks of HarperCollins Christian Publishing, Inc.

The author is represented by Alive Literary Agency, www.aliveliterary.com.

Thomas Nelson titles may be purchased in bulk for educational, business, fundraising, or sales promotional use. For information, please email SpecialMarkets@ThomasNelson.com.

Unless otherwise noted, Scripture quotations are taken from the New King James Version®. Copyright © 1982 by Thomas Nelson. Used by permission. All rights reserved.

Scripture quotations marked BRENTON are taken from *The English Translation of the Septuagint* by Sir Lancelot Charles Lee Brenton (1807–1862), originally published in 1851.

Scripture quotations marked ESV are taken from the ESV® Bible (The Holy Bible, English Standard Version®). Copyright © 2001 by Crossway, a publishing ministry of Good News Publishers. Used by permission. All rights reserved.

Scripture quotations marked KJV are taken from the King James Version. Public domain.

Scripture quotations marked NASB are taken from the New American Standard Bible® (NASB). Copyright © 1960, 1962, 1963, 1968, 1971, 1972, 1973, 1975, 1977, 1995, 2020 by The Lockman Foundation. Used by permission. www.lockman.org

Scripture quotations marked NIV are taken from The Holy Bible, New International Version®, NIV®. Copyright © 1973, 1978, 1984, 2011 by Biblica, Inc.® Used by permission of Zondervan. All rights reserved worldwide. www.Zondervan.com. The "NIV" and "New International Version" are trademarks registered in the United States Patent and Trademark Office by Biblica, Inc.®

Scripture quotations marked NLT are taken from the Holy Bible, New Living Translation. © 1996, 2004, 2015 by Tyndale House Foundation. Used by permission of Tyndale House Publishers, Inc., Carol Stream, Illinois 60188. All rights reserved.

All emphasis in Scripture quotations is added by the author.

Any internet addresses, phone numbers, or company or product information printed in this book are offered as a resource and are not intended in any way to be or to imply an endorsement by Thomas Nelson, nor does Thomas Nelson vouch for the existence, content, or services of these sites, phone numbers, companies, or products beyond the life of this book.

ISBN 978-1-4002-4187-3 (ePub)
ISBN 978-1-4002-4184-2 (HC)

Library of Congress Cataloging-in-Publication Data

Names: Greene, Travis, author.
Title: Are you praying for the wrong thing? : learning to ask what God wants for you, not just what you want / Travis Greene.
Description: Nashville, Tennessee : Nelson Books, [2024] | Summary: "The Bible tells us to pray continually and without ceasing, but what happens when we're waiting for God but discover He's waiting for us? In his first book, pastor and recording artist Travis Greene guides the reader to apply Biblical truths for a fulfilled life"-- Provided by publisher.
Identifiers: LCCN 2023056002 (print) | LCCN 2023056003 (ebook) | ISBN 9781400241842 (hardcover) | ISBN 9781400241873 (ebook)
Subjects: LCSH: Self-actualization (Psychology)--Religious aspects--Christianity. | Prayer.
Classification: LCC BV4598.2 .G744 2024 (print) | LCC BV4598.2 (ebook) | DDC 248.3/2--dc23/eng/20240208
LC record available at https://lccn.loc.gov/2023056002
LC ebook record available at https://lccn.loc.gov/2023056003

Printed in the United States of America

24 25 26 27 28 LBC 5 4 3 2 1

There have been many dreams that started in my heart and eventually found their way into my hands. My boys, the church, this book—all of them have the same common denominator: Jackie. You are a life-giver. Thank you for helping me birth another dream. This book and every other that I'll write is dedicated to you.

Contents

Introduction   ix

ONE: Are You Ready for What You're Praying For?   1

TWO: Catching the Rhythm of Spiritual Discipline   15

THREE: Making God's Dreams Yours   27

FOUR: Shift the Focus from Stuff to Strategy   43

FIVE: Favor Will Always Find the Faithful   65

SIX: Pray for the *Right* People   87

SEVEN: How to Pray When You're Expecting a Miracle   109

EIGHT: Concentrate on What's Left—Not Who Left   131

NINE: When God Calls an Audible   149

TEN: Waiting for God   167

ELEVEN: Amen   181

Acknowledgments   195

Notes   197

About the Author   201

Introduction

My mom stole my first paycheck. I didn't get a cent.

In my early teens I had played organ for a church in Charleston, South Carolina—a little revival for the congregation. I played my heart out. And even back then, I was pretty good. After the church service, I saw the pastor walking over to me. He had an envelope in his hand. I didn't know what was in the envelope, but I could guess. Most important, though, I knew that envelope was for me.

Me! A kid! It was the first time anything like that had ever happened to me. I never knew you could get paid for doing *anything* at church. That was never a thing when I was growing up. When you sang or played in church, it was like an offering to God, not a job. For a church to offer something in return? Unheard of. But here the pastor was, walking toward me—a smile on his face, his arm raised, an envelope in his hand.

And then, just like a linebacker stepping between a quarterback and a wide receiver to bat down a ball, my mom stepped right in front of the pastor, snatched the envelope out of the pastor's grasp, and handed it back to him.

"No, thank you," she told the pastor with a smile. "I got him."

Nearly thirty years later, I still remember that day—remember it almost like it was yesterday. I was disappointed at the time, but she was teaching me. Training me. *I don't want you to ever get caught up in thinking that you minister for money*, she was telling me. *God will bless you.*

Whatever that envelope held, it couldn't have been worth more than that lesson.

Hey, listen, I believe people *should* be compensated for their time and talents. They should be honored for what they do. I believe all of that. And I've been blessed to make a living as a singer and songwriter doing work that countless people would love to do for free. Many folks probably look at my life from afar and some may even feel a little envy. But that lesson never left me. I might be singing in stadiums in Europe or Africa. I might be performing in front of thousands. I might be recording an album that, God willing, will reach millions. But whenever someone who has hired me hands me an envelope, I remember my mom.

"Travis, don't ever get it conflicted," she told me back then (and I still hear her voice now, even if she's three thousand miles away). "You don't do what you do for what's inside that envelope."

And she's right, I don't.

Sometimes I think that's the problem with our prayer life. That's the problem with *my* prayer life. We're praying for what's inside the envelope instead of a deeper relationship with our Creator. We're praying for the gift, not for God.

The Power of Prayer

How often do you pray? Every week? Every day? Do you pray before meals, before bedtime?

We all know that prayer is important. I'm assuming if you're reading this book, you know the value of prayer. Praying to God is mentioned more than three hundred times in the Bible, according to Strong's Concordance, and you won't find a biblical hero who neglected prayer.

But sometimes we forget to pray, don't we? We get busy. We get frustrated. We've got flesh-and-blood people demanding our time and energy, and we turn our attention to them and away from God. We've got bills to pay and deadlines to meet. Prayer can feel, at best, like a luxury and, at worst, like a drain on our precious time.

But when we lose sight of prayer, we lose sight of ourselves in a big way. Everything around us suffers.

Since I'm a pastor, you'd think I'd remember the importance of prayer. But honestly, I've had times in my life when *I've* forgotten too. I've not prayed as much as I should. Sometimes my focus is still on what's inside the envelope. And sometimes, even when I put the time in and my intentions are good, my focus wavers. I can get distracted. I've not connected and communicated with God like He wants me to—like a son with his Father. And in those times, I feel it. God is the source of all life and all hope, and without prayer, I can feel lifeless and hopeless. As a pastor, I've found that preaching without prayer is just words. As an entrepreneur, I've found that life without prayer is life without direction. Without prayer, I can be an inconsiderate husband, an impatient father, an irrational leader, an inconsistent friend.

Open the Bible, and you'll see how important prayer is: Moses begging God to spare his stiff-necked people (Exodus 32:9–14). King David praising God at the very end of his long life (1 Chronicles 29:9–20). Jesus submitting to His Father's will in the garden of Gethsemane (Matthew 26:36–46). These and countless other people prayed to God in times of joy and pain. They prayed in celebration and in submission. They prayed for protection and salvation and connection. "Rejoice always, pray continually, give thanks in all circumstances," the apostle Paul wrote in 1 Thessalonians 5:16–18, "for this is God's will for you in Christ Jesus" (NIV).

But even if you agree with me that prayer is both beautiful *and* necessary, let's tell the truth: It can be frustrating too. Sometimes you feel like your prayers aren't being answered. Or at least not answered the way you'd like. You can be hurting—physically, mentally, emotionally, financially. You can be praying for healing. You can be praying for help. And what do you hear? Crickets. It's as if God's not there, or that He's taking way too much time getting back to you.

You can think to yourself, *Am I doing something wrong? Do I need to pray longer? More often? More sincerely? Should I shout? Whisper? Do I need a special formula? Am I not saying the right words?*

Our world is filled with beautiful prayers written by scholars and saints—prayers for every occasion, for every need.

If you're looking for a book that gives you just the right language to speak to God—the rules for prayer or the rhythm of prayer—this is not a book like that. This is not a book about when to pray, or where, or why, or for how long.

No. This is a book about you.

This is a book about why your prayers go unanswered. It's a book about why your anguished cries to God sometimes seem to go unheard.

Make no mistake: God hears you. He loves you. He wants to do amazing, life-changing things in your life. He wants to give you blessing after blessing after blessing.

But God wants you to take your eyes off the envelope—and put them on Him.

Keep in mind that God's not interested in being a sweet, indulgent, wealthy uncle who hands out twenty-dollar bills whenever you walk by and ask. God is your *Father*, and He doesn't want you just growing up in faith *happy*. He wants you growing up *prepared*.

And that brings us to an uncomfortable truth: praying without intention is just wishful thinking.

When God Says No

I'm a dad of three boys, all under the age of ten. I love them all very much, and I'd do almost anything for them. But I wouldn't give them the keys to my car. I don't care how much they ask or beg or plead. It doesn't matter. Why? Because giving them my keys would be a disaster! Imagine the damage an eight-year-old behind the wheel of an SUV could do (assuming he could even reach the pedals). Letting one of my young sons drive now would be careless, dangerous, and illegal. I don't let them drive, not because I *don't* love them. I don't let them drive because I *do*.

My love manifests in that no. It manifests in me saying to my children, "We need to wait a while." But you know what? If one of my sons shows a lot of interest in cars and driving, I *might* give him a toy car to practice with.

We're not that much different from my boys wanting to drive. Sometimes God tells us no or "not yet" out of love. Sometimes His love for us is expressed in His closing a door or telling us to wait. And sometimes, when we ask for something big, He gives us something small—something we can practice managing.

And sometimes God doesn't give us anything at all. Sometimes He withholds the envelope for a time. Sometimes, like my mom, He understands the lesson is way more important than the gift.

And I'm telling you right now, we should be *thankful* for those times. We might not feel like giving thanks in the middle of our disappointments and disillusionments. But truth is, the difference between a blessing and a burden is preparation. Can you imagine what a burden it'd be for one of my sons to drive a car without being prepared for it? To work the gas and the brake? To pay attention to the stoplights and school-crossing signs? To safely maneuver through traffic? Imagine the burden he'd feel on the road. Imagine the burden he'd feel if he wrecked his father's car.

Let me say it again: The difference between a blessing and a burden is preparation. Any blessing we're given without being prepared for it, we are liable to misuse. We'll devalue it. Mismanage it. It doesn't matter if it's a person, a position, or a possession. If I'm unprepared for it, it'll pull me down, not lift me up. It'll sink me, not save me.

This isn't a how-to prayer book. This is a book about *what* to pray for and how to prepare ourselves for the answers to our prayers. It's about learning to ask what *God* wants for us, not what we want. It's about letting go of unhealthy desires, dead-end dreams, and life-killing relationships. It's about letting go of our spiritual immaturity and growing up. Getting to the point where God can give us the keys to the car.

This book is about asking ourselves if we're praying for the wrong thing—and learning what to do instead. It's about our own disappointment—when we're praying for something and just heard no. And it's about us learning what God was leading to instead, which always turns out to be way better than what we were asking for.

I know how hard it can be when God seems silent. I know what it feels like to hear no. I know what it's like to stare at a closed door. I know what it's like to ask God for just *that one thing* that would make my life so much better, so much easier, so much more fulfilled, and coming away empty. And I know what it's like to have my prayers answered—and then have that answer seemingly snatched away.

Prayer is critical. I can't overstate its value. It's the pipeline to our Creator, the One who gives us life and hope and joy. But sometimes that pipeline seems to go dry, when it feels like God's answers, God's blessings aren't getting through.

I've got news for you. Sometimes the problem isn't God—the source of all good and great things. Often it's your pipes that need fixing.

CHAPTER ONE

Are You Ready for What You're Praying For?

You don't need a car to tour most churches. But I did for this one.

The church wasn't just one building. It wasn't just one campus. This church had buildings spread across the city of Charlotte—most of them new, with glass gleaming and practically sparkling in the February sun.

I rode in an SUV with the church's executive pastor, and he pointed to each church building we passed, explaining what each was for, who it served, and how and when it came to be. He knew his stuff; after all, this guy had been behind most of the buildings we saw—making sure they were paid for and built to specifications and that they fit every possible need the church might have for them.

He'd been behind my visit too. The church had invited me to sing, and I saw all these buildings after a busy Sunday of ministering at multiple services.

I pastor my own church, Forward City, just ninety miles south down I-77 in Columbia, South Carolina. It didn't look anything like this church. Mine looked like a warehouse—which is really what it was. My wife, Jackie, and I preached out of a cramped prefab steel building, which barely had enough room for three hundred people. More than eight hundred people would cram into this building to worship during three services every Sunday. Sometimes it felt as if we didn't have enough room for chairs.

We'd been on the lookout for a new building for a while, but we knew we didn't have the money for one. Each Sunday, that cramped warehouse felt smaller and smaller. And despite all the singing and preaching and giving and saving that went on week after week, it started feeling less like a house of God and more like a prison. And each week I thought to myself, more and more often, *We need more room. If we just had more room, all of our problems would get better. We'd be able to serve more people. We'd be able to serve God better. We just need more room.*

It felt like our church was stuck, unable to move forward.

The Charlotte church I was visiting had exponentially more money, more resources, more people, more everything. So as we drove along, and as I watched these beautiful church buildings pass by, I marveled at how God had blessed this church with so much—and to be honest, I felt a little envy too.

So I turned to my friend, the executive pastor.

"How did you do all this?" I asked. "How is it possible for a new church to have so much?"

My friend smiled a little and said, nonchalantly, "Someone gave us a million dollars."

I don't know exactly what I said or did at that point. Did I do a comical double take? Did I say, "Wow, that's great!"? Did I just smile and turn to look out the window again? I don't remember.

But I remember how I felt. And I felt . . . everything.

I was happy for the church and its windfall. I was inspired and encouraged, knowing that such things can happen to good churches, even if it wasn't happening to mine.

But on top of all those emotions and maybe a dozen others, I was something else.

I was furious.

Growing Pains

I never thought I'd start a church. It was never a goal of mine, never on a bucket list. I was happy doing what I was doing—touring the world and performing. I never saw myself as head-pastor material. I was the guy doing worship music. I was the guy doing youth ministry. I wasn't the guy to lead a whole church, much less plant one.

But one day in 2013, I was in the Atlanta airport, and it hit me: a call to start a church.

I can only describe it as a holy burden—so powerful, so strong. I knew God was asking me to step outside my comfort zone and do something new. Something scary.

The burden was so overwhelming that I called my wife—right there in the airport. I couldn't wait.

"Jackie," I said, "you're not going to believe this. But I think God wants us to start a church."

But Jackie did believe it. "I always knew we were going to start a church," she told me. "I was just waiting on God to tell you."

But how? Where? When?

We prayed about it, and God surprised us again and again. It wasn't long before He pointed us to Columbia, South Carolina. We had no real connection to the city. Even though my parents went to college in Columbia and my dad proposed to my mom there, the city was virtually unknown to me. I'd never even been to a Walmart there. But God kept pointing to that place on the map, and by faith we moved here in 2015. As we thought about a possible name for the church, "Forward City" kept coming up.

That summed up what we wanted our church to stand for. We wanted to be a blessing to the city—to help it in both very tangible and spiritual ways. We wanted the people who filled the church to be able to be blessed and healed too. To move in the direction that God wanted them to go. To pursue Him with all of their hearts. To let go of old hurts and everything that was holding them back. To *move forward*.

Nothing else seemed better, or even close to as good. We felt that it was such a good name that it was probably already being used, so we did a search online. Sure enough, it *had* been used, but it wasn't being used now. A church down in Alabama called itself Forward Church years before. And get this: the lead pastors were named Travis and Jackie.

God's call couldn't be more obvious. We knew that we were doing His will and that we were right where He wanted us to be. And at first, it seemed as though God cleared the way for us. Everything was easy. Exhilarating. *Fun.*

We started holding prayer gatherings in 2016 at the Agape Conference Center in downtown Columbia. By August, we shifted to Sunday morning services. About 630 people showed up that first Sunday in August, and more than a hundred were saved. And with each week, more people came. For the first two years, everything just *worked*.

And then the bottom dropped out.

You could've traced a lot of the church's problems at that time straight from its successes. In the beginning, everything was new and electrifying. We were experimenting—trying new things and excited to see where the Lord was taking us. And we were doing things that no one in Columbia had done in a church setting before. When we moved into that warehouse, we built a stage. We put in a few lights.

And suddenly, it was as if people were pointing to us and saying, "My gosh, you have the best light show in Columbia!" It was a little like we were playing basketball with a four-foot goal; it was easy to dunk.

But after the first two years, we had reference points. We knew what worked *last* year. We knew what worked *last* Easter. And some in the church just wanted to do those same things again. And again.

I didn't want to do those same things. I've always considered myself to be a man of excellence, where good isn't good enough. I had huge goals for our church. I've learned that if you're not moving forward, you're falling behind. If you're not innovating, you're stagnating.

Yeah, I was a nuisance. I wanted everything that we did in Forward City to reflect God's glory and love. I wanted Forward City to serve Columbia in the same way that Christ has served and sacrificed for us. But while I was pushing super-high goals, others wanted to push those goals a little lower. While I wanted our church to be fantastic in everything it did, others felt that *good* was good enough. While I wanted Forward City to move itself forward, others were just more comfortable standing still. Change is hard and uncomfortable. And for a lot of people—understandably—church is meant to be comfortable. And they started grumbling.

And folks weren't just talking—they were *leaving*. These were people I built the church with. These were people who said they wanted to be part of the church forever. But now they weren't happy, and I couldn't pay them enough, or compliment them enough, to stay.

That season was hard. Brutally hard. I never felt like leaving; I'm no quitter. And God was still working in our church. From the outside, Forward City looked like a miracle. But personally, it felt like we were stuck. Like *I* was stuck. I might never have thought about quitting, but I was at a very low point. It wasn't fun anymore. It was a job—a hard, thankless job.

Nothing is more frustrating as a leader than trying to lead with

NOTHING IS MORE FRUSTRATING AS A LEADER THAN TRYING TO LEAD WITH ENTHUSIASM WHEN YOU DON'T HAVE THAT ENTHUSIASM.

enthusiasm when you don't have that enthusiasm. Everybody's unhappy and I know it. Not only are they unhappy, but *I'm* unhappy.

What would make me happy? What would right the ship? *Money.* Resources. Opportunities to do what I wanted to do with that church that required a healthier bank account. That's what I thought during that season. Money might not buy happiness, but it could buy a new building to replace the one we'd far outgrown. It could pay great people to fill our staff. It could provide for all the improvements I wanted to make, all the stuff I wanted to do.

And so I prayed. Man, how I prayed. I prayed for resources. I prayed for people. I prayed for God to give our church a miracle. I knew God could, so why wouldn't He?

But God didn't give us a miracle. He didn't give us what I was praying for.

Maybe I should pray more often, I thought. So I tried it. Didn't work.

Maybe I should pray longer. I tried that too. It didn't work either.

I couldn't figure it out. Here I was, ministering to the city that I was sure God called me to. I was following the burden He'd placed on my heart. Why was God making it so difficult for me?

And that's where I was, mentally and emotionally, when I rode in that SUV in Charlotte—when I toured that gigantic church where money seemed like it was practically falling on them from the sky.

Preparing the Way

Looking back, it's kind of hilarious how upset I was.

"This ain't cool, man," I silently told God during that tour in

Charlotte. "What's going on?! Is it because I'm Black? God, this doesn't feel fair. I never asked to pastor a church! I never asked to move to South Carolina! I'm working my *butt* off, and I have no money, no new building, no joy!"

I could feel myself getting more and more irate. And still I held my private conversation with God, telling Him all the reasons He should be giving me *exactly* what I wanted. "I sing in massive concerts! I don't need to be working day and night in that tiny warehouse! I could be bringing joy to thousands instead of making my staff mad! This is *ridiculous*!" All the while I rode in the SUV, smiling at my friend and fuming at God.

And then, maybe in the space that opened when I took a mental breath, God spoke to me.

What would you do with a million dollars?

I stopped. I had no answer.

"Well," I said, "I'd build something."

Build what?

I didn't know. Something bigger, something better, but outside of that I didn't have any idea. I didn't even know how much a down payment would be.

"I'd hire somebody."

Hire who?

I didn't know who. I didn't even know for what.

"Well, maybe I'd hire a *bunch* of people."

Travis, God said gently, *what would that new staff do?*

And then, in a flash, I realized that I didn't even know what my *current* staff did. Not really. God was asking me basic questions that I didn't have answers for. In that moment—right in that car—God exposed me. He laid me bare.

My heart was full of passion, but I didn't have a plan. I had a wish, but I didn't even know, really, what I was wishing for. I was like a runner at the starting line—shaking out his muscles, stretching out his calves, fired up to start the race—but a runner who forgot his shoes at home.

Money is easy for me, God told me. *I could send whatever resources you want at any moment. But what, Travis, would you do with them? How would you use them?*

I'm not the holdup. You are.

And just like that, I understood. I was praying for the wrong thing!

I was praying for stuff when I should've been praying for the strategy to lead. I wanted miracles when I should've been asking God to help me manage what I'd already been given. I wanted God's favor in the future when I should've been focusing on faithfulness in the present. I was begging for more people when I should've been examining a better process.

> I WANTED GOD'S FAVOR IN THE FUTURE WHEN I SHOULD'VE BEEN FOCUSING ON FAITHFULNESS IN THE PRESENT.

What I should've been praying for wasn't more resources or staffing or even a new building; I should've been praying for maximizing what our church already had. If God had given me what I had been praying for, I wouldn't have known how to use it. I would've wasted His gift and squandered His resources. Without a strong culture and a healthy working environment, any extra resources wouldn't be maximized. Without the right systems and a good strategy in place, extra staff wouldn't fit well. A bigger building would just be a breeding ground for bigger issues. I believe that a wise philosopher of this age—Biggie Smalls—had it right: "Mo money mo problems."[1]

God is great. He can do *anything*. But He also gave us free will and the ability to choose how we use all those gifts He's given us. So before we ask Him to pour out more blessings and bounty for us, we must ask ourselves two critical questions: One, What am I doing with the gifts God has already given me? And two, What would I do with more?

That SUV ride in Charlotte changed my life. I kept a picture from that day so I could mark the moment. God altered my whole outlook that day, and I came back to Columbia a different person. My mind was renewed. I saw everything differently.

How I changed reminds me of a friend of mine. She has an extreme phobia of germs. Everything in her life—everything around her—must be incredibly clean. You walk into her house and it's spotless. I never see a speck of dirt. But she will. She'll notice a smudge on the counter or a vent that needs to be cleaned out—stuff that you or I wouldn't even be able to see. And she'll decide that it must be fixed right then.

That's the way her mind is wired. She sees the world differently. She sees things that other people can't. And in my own way, that's what happened to me.

I remember coming back from Charlotte and walking into our church. It was the same church I had walked out of just a day before. It was as familiar as our family home or a friendly face. But to me it looked different. Suddenly I could see it all so much more clearly. I saw all the ways that we could make it *better*—not with more money, not with more staff or moving to a new location, but with what we had *now*. I saw cracks in the wall and said, "We need to fill in the cracks and paint." I saw a cluttered closet and said, "This needs to be organized." I wanted the chairs in the sanctuary to be lined up perfectly. I wanted our services to be even more moving. I wanted to maximize every nook, every cranny, every square foot in that church. I didn't want to be the one to blame for God not being able to do what He wanted to do. I didn't want to be the holdup.

When I spoke to my staff after my trip to Charlotte, I immediately shared my vision with them.

"Listen, I know we've been looking at all of our needs," I said. "We need a new building, we need this, we need that. But from here on out, we're not going to look at buildings. We're not going to focus on moving. We're going to focus on *maximizing* what we have.

"If we get great at what we do, God will give us what we need."

So that's what we focused on: what we had, not what we thought we needed. From that day forward, that's been our church's focus. When we stopped focusing on what we thought God needed to do for *us* and instead focused on what *we* needed to do for God—how we were doing ministry for Him—doors started opening. As I write this, we're settling into a new forty-four-thousand-square-foot building—an old Best Buy with plenty of space inside and out. We've got the largest indoor playground in the area. Our youth room is bigger than our entire sanctuary was in the old building. We have room for one thousand worshippers—and with our online ministry, we're reaching literally thousands more each week.

God has been good to us. But as the saying goes, God is good all the time. And for all the gifts our church has received from Him in the past few years, His biggest gift wasn't the building; it wasn't the resources He provided. It was in what He whispered to me in that SUV in 2019. Those words changed me.

God Is in the Details

I'm astounded by how often the Bible talks about preparation and using your resources and your talents wisely. One of my favorites, found in Matthew 25, is even called the parable of the talents.

The *talents* that Jesus was talking about weren't the same as what we think of. He wasn't talking about how athletic you are or how smart you are or how well you cook. Back in Christ's day, a talent was a unit of weight, but that unit was essentially used to measure ludicrous amounts of wealth. (For instance, in 1 Kings 10:10 the queen of Sheba is said to have given Solomon 120 talents of gold.)

So when Jesus talked about talents, He was really talking about *money*. And the parable goes something like this:

The kingdom of heaven is like a rich man going far away who didn't want his money to just sit there while he was gone. So he called his servants in, divvied up his wealth, and gave that money to each of his servants—based on their abilities—to take care of while he was gone.

The first servant was given, say, $500,000. That servant promptly invested that money, and by the time his employer returned, he had a million bucks to give him. His boss was incredibly happy with him. "Well done, good and faithful servant," he told him. "You were faithful over a few things. I will make you ruler over *many* things. Enter into the joy of your lord."

The second servant was given $200,000. He invested it too. And sure enough, when his employer came back, the money had doubled as well—up to $400,000. When his boss saw this, he praised this second servant just as he had the first. "Well done, good and faithful servant," he said. And he put him in charge of a lot more too.

But the third servant, when he went before his boss, said (and I'm paraphrasing here), "Sir, I knew you were a hard guy to please. You reap what you've not sown and gather where you've not scattered seed. I knew if I screwed up, you'd take it out on me. So I didn't take any chances. I buried your talent in the ground, and here it is. Now you can have what's yours."

His employer was furious. "You wicked and lazy servant!" he told him. "You knew that I reap where I have not sown and gather where I have not scattered seed! You knew I was looking to get that money back with interest! I didn't ask you to take a chance with crypto! I didn't ask you to buy junk bonds! But you should've at least put it in the bank, so that when I came back, I would've had that money and a little interest besides!" So he took away the $100,000 from that third servant and gave it to the first. Because he knew that the first servant would know what to do with it.

"Enter into the joy of your lord," the rich man told his two faithful servants. The criteria for entering into that joy isn't just about being good. It's about being faithful—and that includes being faithful stewards of all our *talents*—the resources we're given and our God-given abilities too—that we've been entrusted with. Faithfulness matters. And if we're faithful with a little, that prepares and qualifies us for more. How we treat a little will determine how much our own divine Lord will entrust us with. And how we handle what we have, whether little or much, tells God—and us—a lot about how we'll handle a lot.

My uncle is a little like the rich man from Jesus' parable. He was a hotshot accountant who worked for everybody who was anybody, it seems—from Fortune 500 companies to NBA players. He was always very serious and very focused. That third servant might've called him a hard guy to please. Growing up, the main things I knew about my uncle were that he was really smart and really rich.

When I was in college, some friends of mine and I wanted to start a clothing line. But of course, none of us had any money. So as we were making plans, I reached out to my uncle and asked him if he'd be interested in investing in our company—and give a bunch of young, hungry, and creative guys a chance.

Well, I gave him my pitch, and my uncle seemed open to the idea. But then he threw in this qualifier that, for a second, felt a little like cold water on the whole operation: He wanted us to keep receipts for every penny we spent. Every single cent.

Don't you trust us? part of me wondered at the time. But then he told me something that I've never forgotten: "If you take care of the pennies, the dollars will take care of themselves."

That's a wise man right there. What he said was a game changer—even if it didn't change me immediately. I'm not wired to count every penny. I struggle dealing with details. I'm more of a big picture guy. But that doesn't change the brilliance of what my uncle told me. Those pennies *are* important—not just to my uncle but to God too.

I'm a dreamer. I wouldn't have had the success I've had if I wasn't. Dreams are important. If you ask me, dreams are critical. God wants you to dream big—because it's only in following those dreams that you can tap that potential that God put inside you. God created you—*you*—for a purpose. He wants you to be a part of His glorious song.

But He wants you to take care of the pennies too.

All that He's done for you? He can do more. *Much* more. But God wants to see what you do with what He's already handed to you. And while it's fine to ask for what you want and what you need, the more important ask is this: ask for His help to maximize what you already have.

Stuck in a cubicle and think you deserve that corner office? Maybe. But do the very best work in that cubicle you can. Excel in everything you're asked to do. Put in the time. Push yourself to greatness—because you can be great wherever you are, whatever you do.

Stuck on the second team and think the coach hates you? Doesn't matter. Work as hard in practice as you do during the game. Put the extra reps in to hone your skills. Hustle with each trip down the court, through each play, during each at-bat. Push yourself to maximize the chances you're given.

Struggling in a relationship? Feel like you're taken for granted? It happens, for sure. But keep doing your best for those you care for. Teach your children well. Love your spouse like you'd like to be loved. Give that relationship your very best.

STRIVE FOR EXCELLENCE. AIM TO BE THE PERSON THAT GOD CREATED YOU TO BE.

In every job, every day, every circumstance of life, maximize. Strive for excellence. Aim to be the person that God created you to be.

Now, here's the hard truth: While oftentimes maximizing your gifts can and will bring you the success you long for or the appreciation you deserve, it doesn't *always* happen. Everyone around you—your bosses, your teachers, your coaches, your family—is just as imperfect as you are. Sometimes, no matter how hard you work, you'll be overlooked. Sometimes, no matter how hard you try, you'll be taken for granted. You'll be taken advantage of. God doesn't guarantee us that corner office. And God never promises that His dreams for us are the same as ours.

But God knows when you have stewarded His gifts well. And when you maximize what little you have been given, the Lord will give you more. It's not always in the way that you want or the way you expect or even in the way you think you need, but believe me—God knows when you've been taking care of the pennies. He knows when you've been a good and faithful servant, even if the world is slow to see it, or never sees it.

How do you go about maximizing those gifts? What's the first step?

For that, you need a plan. And before you can stop praying for the wrong thing, you need to learn how to rethink prayer itself.

CHAPTER TWO

Catching the Rhythm of Spiritual Discipline

How do you pray for the right thing? You have to get closer to God.

How do you get closer to God? Great question. People have been thinking about that since Adam and Eve got kicked out of the garden of Eden.

If Adam and Eve hadn't messed up so bad right in the beginning, it'd be easy to get to know God. He was close to us then. In Genesis 3:8, we're told He was "walking in the garden in the cool of the day." The message there is obvious: Adam and Eve were close to God, and God was close to them. It didn't take work. It didn't take discipline.

But then came the snake and the fruit and the rebellion, and God locked us out of Eden. Humanity fell into sin, and just like that, we were separated from the Lord. He still loves us. He loves us like crazy. But just as God cursed Adam, telling him he'd need to toil just to get a little food from the ground (Genesis 3:17–19), it often feels like He makes us work harder to get our spiritual nourishment from Him too.

Adam and Eve weren't asked to pray or fast or observe the Sabbath. But the Bible asks us to do all those things now.

We can—and do—get closer to the Almighty. And a lot of us do that through what have become known as *spiritual disciplines*.

And while I'm sure that some Christian experts could rattle off dozens of disciplines, going into exhaustive—and exhausting— detail on each one, I really just want to tell you about five here. These are five that I try to concentrate on: prayer, fasting, reading the Bible, observing the Sabbath, and getting away to find spiritual space. I've found these five to be critical in my own relationship with God.

And we begin with the big one—where, in my opinion, all relationships with God begin: prayer.

Prayer

Then He spoke a parable to them, that men
always ought to pray and not lose heart.
—LUKE 18:1

This is so obvious, but it's so important. You can't know what God's word is for you without asking Him.

David is one of the Bible's best role models for prayer. He praised God in prayer (Psalm 145, for instance). He prayed for guidance (1 Samuel 23:1–2). He prayed for miraculous healing for his own sick son (2 Samuel 12:16)—a prayer that was, unfortunately, not answered. But still David prayed—in good times and bad, in joy and in suffering. Most of his psalms are prayers. In Psalm 5 the king suggested that it was one of the first things he did when he woke up.

My voice You shall hear in the morning, O LORD;
In the morning I will direct it to You,
And I will look up.

—verse 3

If it was good enough for David, it's good enough for me.

I typically start my days at 6 a.m., and the very first thing I do is pray. It's so important to talk with God first thing—to lean into Him almost the moment you open your eyes.

Now, I know that's not always possible. Sometimes circumstances force me to change that up. I might need to respond to an emergency or deal with something at 6:15 a.m., which can cut short or delay my prayer time. But most days of the week, I'm praying by 6 a.m. I pray for the day ahead. The week ahead. The specific challenges that I'm facing right now.

But at the beginning of the year, I pray for *seasonal* instruction too. *Hey, God,* I ask. *What does this year look like for You? What do You have in mind for me? What is Your focus?*

In 2023, for instance, God said, *Travis, you need to lock in. You need to concentrate on the church. You need to focus on staffing. You need to focus on leaders. You need to focus on coaching.*

So I have. This year has been about all those elements, as we try to keep Forward City moving forward. That's my *seasonal* instruction. It might be different next year. Next year, God might want me to concentrate more on, say, a new album or a new tour. But whatever that instruction may be in the future, I know what I'm supposed to be doing this year, and that's what I concentrate on. Once I have that seasonal word, it's so much easier to say no to some of those shiny new things that might come along—like a thirty-city tour. No matter how lucrative it is, if God didn't instruct me to do it, it just doesn't make sense for that season. I don't have to go back and ask God, "Hey, is this from You?" Because it doesn't match the seasonal word that I have. Listening for and obeying God's instruction has helped me to stay focused on God's grid.

> LISTENING FOR AND OBEYING GOD'S INSTRUCTION HAS HELPED ME TO STAY FOCUSED ON GOD'S GRID.

That dual prayer—to pray for the day and pray for the season—is important for everybody. We need to talk with God about the day and about the year. And really, we should be talking with Him about *everything*.

Have you asked God about His instruction for you lately? Have you prayed for His direction? Or are you walking forward blindly? Talk to Him. Pray.

God, what would You like me to do this month? This year? How can I be Your instrument? How can I be Your servant?

He has plans for you. He says so. "'For I know the plans I have for you,' declares the LORD, 'plans to prosper you and not to harm you, plans to give you hope and a future'" (Jeremiah 29:11 NIV).

That verse doesn't mean He'll give you everything you want. But follow Him, and He'll give you what *to* want. Lean into His plans, His instruction. Do what He wants you to do, and you'll find peace. Hope. Your future.

Fasting

> So we fasted and implored our God for
> this, and He answered our prayer.
> —EZRA 8:23

A lot of Christians ignore this facet of faith. It feels too strict, too severe. It doesn't always need to be about food. You can fast from television, social media. If there's something in your life that's pulling you away from your relationship with God, it might be smart to do without it for a while. But in the Bible, fasting was about food. It was about denying yourself the very thing that your body needs to keep going.

Prayer and fasting are often linked in Scripture. Esther fasted. David fasted. *Jesus*—the Son of God Himself—fasted. In Acts 13 Paul and Barnabas were sent off to spread the Word of God—their own instruction from the Almighty—after prayer and fasting. Each time Paul and Barnabas appointed new leaders and elders for the church, they committed them through prayer and fasting.

We should fast because Jesus did. And that's why we've made fasting part of the rhythm of our church. We encourage our attendees to fast. We *require* our leaders to fast. Every year, we start with a liquid-only fast for twenty-one days. Additionally, our pastors, elders, prayer team, and staff go on a three-day fast at the beginning of each month. And when I fast, I'll cut out something else too. Social media, maybe. Or TV. Something that all too often becomes an escape and might compete for attention with God.

Fasting, like everything, should start with prayer. We need to ask God to give us strength while we're fasting—and for Him to teach us while we're fasting. How long should you fast? Depends. As I said, we engage in multi-week fasts at Forward City, but the Bible doesn't tell us that a fast counts only if it's forty days long. Judges 20 talks about partial-day fasts, where you fast until sunset. In Esther 4, Queen Esther fasted for three days and asked the Jewish people of Susa to do so as well.

I believe that fasting adds weight to our prayers—not how God hears our prayer but how we pray. I find that when I fast, I just have more clarity, more focus. Hey, the world is noisy. So many things are shouting at us every day. Fasting helps amplify the right voice. Helps me hear Him more clearly. It helps me to be laser focused on what I need to do. My own pastor often says, "You can pray without fasting, but you can't fast without praying."

I also think that the process of fasting can strengthen the spirit even as it weakens the body. Look at Matthew 4, when Jesus was being tempted by the devil in the wilderness. Matthew tells us that Jesus was led into the wilderness specifically to be tempted by the devil. And once He was there, He started fasting. For forty days and forty nights He fasted, and only then did Satan come to Him. And what was the first temptation Jesus faced? *Food.*

"If You are the Son of God," Satan told Jesus, "command that these stones become bread."

The Bible tells us that Jesus was hungry, as any of us would've been after forty days without food. Doctors say that the human body, if it doesn't get outside nutrients for a while, starts feeding on itself. "The body works to fight starvation by producing glucose and breaking down fatty tissue," Verywell Health says. "In later stages, it breaks down muscle."[1]

People feel weak. They can feel cold—even in the Judean wilderness, the desert. We know that the fast took a lot out of Jesus, because when His time in the wilderness was over, angels themselves came to minister to Him. "All right," I imagine they said, "You really need some *food.*"

The devil attacked Jesus when He was physically at His weakest, which feels totally unfair. Keep in mind, Jesus' time in the wilderness was a heavyweight spiritual bout, a showdown with Lucifer—who was once one of God's most beautiful and beloved angels before he rebelled—and the Son of God Himself. Satan's assault on Jesus was like a World Wrestling Entertainment (WWE) cheat—hitting Jesus with a folding chair while the Son of God was tying His shoe.

But while Jesus might've been starving physically, He was filled spiritually. Listen to what Jesus said: "It is written, 'Man shall not live by bread alone, but by every word that proceeds from the mouth of God'" (Matthew 4:4). *Man shall not live by bread alone.* When we fast, we remind ourselves of that core truth. We might be hungry, but that very hunger helps us to focus on what should be our real sustenance. It reminds us of the people all around us—halfway around the globe or halfway down the block—who never have enough to eat. With each hunger pang, it reminds us of our own human frailty and our need for a Savior. And because of all

> WHEN WE FAST PROPERLY— PACKAGING IT WITH PRAYER AND COMMITMENT—OUR HUNGER FOR FOOD BECOMES A HUNGER FOR CHRIST.

these things, fasting draws us closer to God. When we fast properly—packaging it with prayer and commitment—our hunger for food becomes a hunger for Christ.

Reading the Bible

All Scripture is God-breathed and is useful for teaching, rebuking, correcting and training in righteousness, so that the servant of God may be thoroughly equipped for every good work.

—2 TIMOTHY 3:16–17 (NIV)

You can't just read the Bible. You gotta *read the Bible.*

I tell that to people a lot, and it means just this: When you read Scripture, you can't just let the words flow past your eyes like fish in a stream. You've got to grab them. Catch them. Hold them in your heart and let them wriggle there. They're too precious and way too important to let pass without thinking about what you're reading—and praying about it too.

George Müller was a famous Christian evangelist and social worker in nineteenth-century England, running the Ashley Down orphanage in Bristol and launching more than one hundred schools for the poor. He was famous for his prayer life, but he also realized that prayer went hand in hand with reading and contemplating Scripture. Here's what he wrote about it:

> Before this time my practice had been, at least for ten years previously, as an habitual thing, to give myself to prayer, after having dressed the morning. Now I saw, that the most important thing I had to do was to give myself to the reading of the Word of God and to meditation on it, that thus my heart might be comforted, encouraged, warned, reproved, instructed. . . . I began therefore, to meditate on the New Testament, from the beginning, early in the morning.
>
> The first thing I did, after having asked in a few words the Lord's blessing upon His precious Word, was to begin to meditate on the Word of God; searching, as it were, into every verse, to get blessing out of it; not for the sake of the public ministry of the Word; not for the sake of preaching on what I had meditated upon; but for the sake of obtaining food for my own soul.[2]

I absolutely relate to that. I love reading Scripture—absolutely love it. Five days a week, I'm not reading the Bible to study up for a message. I'm just reading for the sake of my spiritual life—for the sake, as Müller said, of getting food for my soul. I read the Bible with a red pen nearby, and my Bible is filled with underlined words and circled phrases and notes. Read this book, and you'll probably see how much I love that one. God's stories are amazing. They come alive for me. And I think you'll find that, the more you read the Bible, the more it'll come alive for you too. The Bible is so rich and so vibrant and so compelling.

Observing the Sabbath

Come to Me, all you who labor and are
heavy laden, and I will give you rest.

—MATTHEW 11:28

We'll talk more in-depth about this concept later in this book. But briefly, if our own packed schedules and insane pace distract us from God and His instruction, it only makes sense that slowing down could help counter that. If we decide to rest instead of rush, that can help us hear God's instruction more clearly.

And if common sense isn't enough to convince us to push pause on our busy lives on occasion, God Himself tells us to.

Jesus said in Mark 2:27 that "the Sabbath was made for man, and not man for the Sabbath." Christ was telling a high priest why He and His disciples were picking heads of grain, but this is another verse that we're liable to misinterpret if we're not careful. Some people look at this and say, "See? Jesus didn't rest on the Sabbath. That means I can put in a full workday right after church." But that's not what Jesus said.

The Sabbath was made for man. God not only created the Sabbath but He also created it for *us.* Now, why would He do that? Just so we could watch football? I don't think so. He knows us. He

> GOD NOT ONLY CREATED THE SABBATH BUT HE ALSO CREATED IT FOR US. HE KNOWS US. HE MADE US. AND HE UNDERSTANDS — WAY BETTER THAN WE DO SOMETIMES — THAT WE ALL NEED REST.

made us. And He understands—way better than we do sometimes—that we all need rest.

Taking a Sabbath in the Bible was not a request.

Getting Away

And He said to them, "Come aside by yourselves
to a deserted place and rest a while."

—MARK 6:31

We all know that getting away—separating yourself physically and mentally from your day-to-day life—can be pretty important. A little downtime makes a big difference. If I'm struggling with writer's block in my musical career, I try to get away. I travel. Maybe I go to a concert featuring someone from a different genre. *Separation* can bring you to a place of *inspiration*.

I think that's true spiritually too.

Let's go back to the Bible for a minute. Look at almost any biblical hero you want to, and you'll find that they invariably took some downtime to receive their own words of instruction. They separated themselves, physically and mentally, from the responsibilities and demands of their day-to-day lives. They moved, often literally, into a different space so they could hear God better.

Think about Moses, who separated himself from all the Hebrews he was leading through the wilderness to scale another mountain—this time, Mount Sinai. Remember, around six hundred thousand "footmen" followed Moses out of Egypt (Numbers 11:21 BRENTON). Count women and children and the elderly, and that number balloons. Moses was leading a huge nation around in the wilderness. He had an overwhelming amount of responsibilities. But to talk with God, he left all these people and all his duties and headed out alone. And there Moses received not just *his* instruction but commandments for all of us to follow.

Even Jesus Himself, in the garden of Gethsemane, separated Himself from His closest followers. "You stay here while I go over there to pray," Jesus told them.

Again and again, the people who followed God the most sincerely had their most profound encounters with the Almighty in the quiet spaces they could carve out. They went away—up mountains, into gardens, through the wilderness. They sought God in silent spots. How can we hope to hear the Lord's still, small voice if we don't silence our own cell phones and muzzle our own calendars? How can we imagine we're going to encounter our invisible Creator when we fill our worlds with so many visible distractions?

Even back then, before Wi-Fi and smart TVs, God knew we needed to take time, to find space, to carve out a little silence to encounter Him. How much more must we need it today?

Silence is the space where we can listen. Silence is the place where we can ask questions . . . and have the ability to hear the answers.

So in this silence, let me ask a few questions of you.

What do you do first thing in the morning? Do you look at your phone? Drag yourself down to the kitchen and pour yourself some cereal? Panic because you're already late for the day?

Let me encourage you, if you don't do so already, to make the first words you speak be to God. Talk to Him. Pray. Let the first words you read be from the Bible. Read. Ask God to fill your day with His meaning. Ask God to guide you where He wants to take you. Ask Him to give you His instruction.

What is God's instruction? Glad you asked.

CHAPTER THREE

Making God's Dreams Yours

Psalm 37:4 is one of the most misquoted verses in the Bible.

The verse is simple: "Delight yourself also in the LORD, and He shall give you the desires of your heart." Plenty of people take that to mean that God is like a genie or Santa Claus. We climb up on His lap and ask for something—a new Land Rover or a pair of designer shoes—and He'll give it to us. Why? Because we *want* it, that's why.

And it leads to a lot of frustrated Christians.

I believe in the power of prayer, absolutely. I believe that God wants you to be happy. He wants to give you joy and pleasure. He wants to give you, honestly, your heart's desires.

But here's the catch: The number one desire of your heart must be . . . God. Not a faster car. Not a bigger house. Not fame or fortune or even happiness. He has to be our number one desire.

And a funny thing happens when you truly put God at the center of your life. His desires become your desires.

It's not that our own desires—our own wants and needs—are bad things. Sometimes they're very good things, even very necessary things. We might pray for a new job. We might pray for the ability to move into a better, safer neighborhood. We can ask God for what seem to be completely reasonable things in our lives. And yet every month, we struggle to pay the bills. Every month we might wonder why we have the same fights with our kids, spouses, or parents. We pray and pray, and the silence just gets thicker. And as time goes on, we grow more disappointed, more frustrated.

So we wonder, *Why isn't He giving us what we want? Why don't we have the desires of our heart?* "God *knows* what I want," we say. "Isn't it about time He gave it to me?"

But if you look closely, there's nothing in the Bible that says He's going to give you what you want. Absolutely nothing. If you look closer at the verse—or any verse that the world claims means that God will reach into a magic bag and hand you whatever you ask for—you'll see that's not what the Scriptures say.

Most people concentrate on the last half of Psalm 37:4, that He'll give you the desires of your heart. But what does the "delight yourself also in the LORD" mean? Look at the surrounding verses:

> Trust in the LORD, and do good;
> Dwell in the land, and feed on His faithfulness.
> Delight yourself also in the LORD,
> And He shall give you the desires of your heart.
> Commit your way to the LORD,
> Trust also in Him,
> And He shall bring it to pass.
> He shall bring forth your righteousness as the light,
> And your justice as the noonday.
>
> —Psalm 37:3–6

"Feed on His faithfulness," David told us. "Commit your way to the LORD." These are all verses that point to a deep relationship and understanding of God. David was talking about more than saying grace at dinner. He was talking about a whole body, whole mind, whole heart connection with our Creator. And that connection inevitably means us telling Him, "Hey, God, I want what You want." It means that we want His desires to be our desires.

Listen up, because this is important: The Bible never says that God will give you what you want. He'll give you what *to* want.

That's so key. If we're really feeding on God's faithfulness and committing our ways to God, our hearts' desires align with His.

Think of it like this: Aligning our desires can be a little like using a pair of binoculars. There's nothing wrong with focusing on our own close-up needs sometimes. There's a place for that. But everything else— the big picture—is all fuzzy. God wants us to go past our own desires, those trees right in front of our faces, and focus on what's beyond. His forests. His mountains. The horizon He made for us. He wants us to see the big picture—the people He designed us to be. And when we zoom in on those trees twenty-five feet away, as important as they might seem right now, we can't really see where God wants to take us.

Where does God want to take you? Do you know? Are you like I was on that trip to Charlotte, asking for blessings that I had no idea how I would even use?

As you pray for what you want and need today—those trees of desire right in front of you— pray for God to adjust your focus too. Pray for Him to help you see what He wants you to see, and what He wants you to be, not just what you want from Him. And when you see it, your breath will be taken away. Because His plans for you are far more glorious and satisfying than your own plans. Sure, it might not be in His plans to make you rich or comfortable. But will those plans be filled with joy?

> PRAY FOR HIM TO HELP YOU SEE WHAT HE WANTS YOU TO SEE, AND WHAT HE WANTS YOU TO BE, NOT JUST WHAT YOU WANT FROM HIM.

Satisfaction? You bet. Because when we follow God's plan, we're doing what we were made to do. And doing what we were made to do is the only way to real joy.

When I think about Psalm 37:4, it's good to pair it with Romans 12:1–2. It's kind of like the B clause for the earlier verse—a way to put it in context. Paul wrote:

> I beseech you therefore, brethren, by the mercies of God, that you present your bodies a living sacrifice, holy, acceptable to God, which is your reasonable service. And do not be conformed to this world, but be transformed by the renewing of your mind, that you may prove what is that good and acceptable and perfect will of God. (KJV)

Paul was telling us that we need to give ourselves to God—body, mind, and spirit. Real worship is about that sacrifice. And verse 2— well, it's become one of my favorite verses in the entire Bible. "Do not be conformed to the world," Paul said. "Be *transformed* by the renewing of your mind."

Paul was saying that you won't even know the will of God until your mind is transformed. Without that renewed mind, without that transformation, you're just guessing.

That time in Charlotte was a transformational moment for me. As I was being driven across that church campus, I was in a place of conformity. *Why can't my church be this big? This successful?* But when God spoke to me, it transformed my whole way of thinking. Every story that I'll relate in this book represents a transformational moment in my life. I was thinking one thing, and then God showed me another way of thinking.

Life is just as much about unlearning as learning. We must unlearn the lessons that the world tries to pound into us and uncover what God's trying to teach us. He's after transformation. And I've found that in every area of my life—business, music, leadership—the quicker I allowed myself to perceive God's truth, the quicker, and the more, I was transformed. And the more I was transformed, the greater my capacity has been for whatever God desires to do through me.

I was a military brat growing up. My dad was an air force chaplain. Every day, he ministered to men and women in the military, whether they were just planning to be in the service for a couple of years or make a career out of it. And while every single person who came to my dad for help was unique, all of them shared one experience with him: basic training. Boot camp.

Every branch of the military has its own version of boot camp, and it's changed a lot since my dad took part in it. But its purpose is still the same: to prepare you for military service physically, mentally, and emotionally. You wake up before dawn. You're stripped of most of the comforts you're used to. You push yourself through countless drills. You learn the ins and outs of military life—all while a drill sergeant is pushing you to be stronger, faster, *better*. And while basic training is meant to teach you those basics of military life—making sure you have the core tools you'll need to succeed—it's about more than that. According to former Navy SEAL Steve Smith, "Boot camp is mostly a mind game. It's designed to take the civilian out of you and replace it with a top-notch military service member."[1] It's all about transforming you from what you were and into what the military wants and needs you to be.

Sometimes unanswered prayer can be a little like boot camp. In the military, you become a "living sacrifice," willingly putting yourself in harm's way to protect and serve your country and the people who live there. But to truly serve them, you have to become more than an individual: you have to become a tool in your country's hand. The same goes with God. He made you unique. He made you special. But

He made you for a *purpose*. And for you to find that purpose—to be transformed into the person that God wants you to be—you can't just stay focused on your own selfish desires. You've got to move into a place where what you want is what God wants. And you can't be transformed without a little pain.

And honestly, without being transformed, you don't even *want* God to give you what you want. Because what we want is sometimes the very last thing we should get! Sometimes we're simply not ready for it.

Think about it like this: Remember in middle school or high school when you first saw that boy or girl that you thought was amazing? The person you thought would surely be your one true love, the person who'd make your life complete? We thought the sun rose and set with that boy or girl. But sooner or later, most of us learned that the sun had nothing to do with that person—and love sure didn't. And then, twenty or thirty years later, if we see that person on the street or in a restaurant, we're like, "Thank *God*. Thank God I didn't get what I wanted back then."

Probably most of us have plenty of examples of times when we didn't get what we wanted—and not getting those things turned out to be a blessing. Think about your own life; I bet you can recall one or two examples right now. We all think we know what we want. But without God, we don't know what *to* want.

Hearing Instruction

Psalm 37:4 is one tiny snippet of one of the Bible's most fascinating and varied books. The poems and prayers in Psalms were meant to be sung. And just like songs today, they run the gamut of human emotion and expression. They praise God. They encourage. They cry out for help.

Psalms is a book full of laughter and tears, sorrow and joy. It's funny that Psalm 37:4 has been so misused, when you think about it. Taken out of context, it contradicts what you read in the rest of the book.

The psalms don't promise easy money or an easy life. Often it's exactly the opposite. The psalmists frequently begged for guidance and understanding—begged God to teach them what to want:

- Make me walk in the path of Your commandments, for I delight in it. (Psalm 119:35)
- How precious also are your thoughts to me, O God! How great is the sum of them! (Psalm 139:17)
- Let the words of my mouth and the meditation of my heart be acceptable in your sight, O LORD, my strength and my Redeemer. (Psalm 19:14)

And David often talked about the importance of God's *instruction*:

- In Psalm 16:7, he said he would "praise the LORD, who counsels me" (NIV).
- In Psalm 19, he wrote at length about the beauty of God's laws and instructions: "The judgments of the LORD are true and righteous altogether. More to be desired are they than gold, yea, than much fine gold; sweeter also than honey and the honeycomb" (verses 9–10).
- Proverbs, most of which is said to have been written by David's son Solomon, is even more specific: "Whoever gives heed to instruction prospers, and blessed is the one who trusts in the LORD" (16:20 NIV).

That's powerful. Instruction, the Bible tells us, is *life* (Proverbs 4:13). Whenever God gives you instruction—an idea of what you should be doing and how you should be doing it—that's something you should steward well.

I believe that instruction goes beyond what is laid down in the Bible. We're not just talking about scriptures that tell us how we should live our lives and treat people around us (though those are, of course, important too). I believe that God has individual instruction for each one of us—plans for how we, individually, are to go about our lives and lean into God's work for us. "For I know the plans I have for you, plans for welfare and not for evil, to give you a future and a hope" (Jeremiah 29:11 ESV).

We need to be good stewards of those plans, of that God-given instruction. But I want to be very specific here: I'm talking about *God's* plan, not ours. We're not supposed to steward selfish dreams that stand apart from God; instead, we should steward the instruction God has given us.

It's so easy to get the two mixed up. It's so easy to mistake our heart's desires for God's. I do it sometimes too. But if you just push pause for a minute and think, you can tell the difference.

When you're stewarding a word from God—when your own plans are aligned with His—there's a certain rest and joy that comes with that, even if those plans involve a lot of hard work. Sometimes we have seasons where we suffer. We all have times in our lives when we struggle, and we need to push through them. Life is *hard*. Sometimes it can feel unbearably hard. But if it's hard all the time—if you're not finding any joy in your life at all—that's something else. We can work hard and find joy in it. We can struggle day to day and still feel satisfaction in it, because we know we're following God's path. We know that He's leading us not only where He wants us to go but where, deep down, we know we're *supposed* to go.

We all have dreams. We all have plans. We all have desires born of our own selfish hearts. But if they're not in line with God's instruction for our lives, it's going to be a heavy yoke indeed. And sometimes it's going to be simply impossible. If you're trying to carry your own dreams without God's blessing, you'll struggle with every step.

Countless young men would love to become professional basketball players. They might have told themselves that, if they just work hard enough, they can do it. They might go to the gym or playground and take a thousand shots a day to make that dream—that heart's desire—come true.

And while all that hard work can pay plenty of dividends, let's be real: If the NBA isn't part of God's plan for your life, it's going to be hard to achieve. I'd love to be a professional basketball player too—but man, at the end of the day, I'm five foot eight. There's one player every fifteen years who makes it to the NBA if they're less than six feet tall. I could practice my jump shot for twelve hours a day, and I'm *still* not making it to the NBA. It's not part of God's plan for me.

God may not give you the desires of your heart. But He will give you the desires of His. And if you follow Him dutifully and faithfully and relentlessly, He'll give you what *to* want. Once you know the desire that God has for you—once you discern His plan—that's what you steward. That's what you cultivate. Your mind is renewed. You've been transformed. You won't have to guess what God wants for your life: you'll know.

Either we're guided or we're guessing.

Sour Milk

I've sometimes lived in that "guessing" space. Honestly, it can be a challenge. I've had seasons when I didn't like who I was. I knew I wasn't giving my kids my best. I wasn't being the husband that Jackie needed me to be. I was irritable. I was tired. I was frustrated. I've walked through whole seasons of my life like that. And for me, that's when I had to push pause for a minute. Working backward, I had to ask myself, *Am I living in God's plan for my life?*

When the answer is no, you've got to consider why. I think it comes down to two basic problems: (1) you didn't know what God's instruction was for you in the first place or (2) you're living on *expired* instruction.

That's confusing, right? How can God's instruction expire? If you knew what God had in mind for you last year, wouldn't that be what He'd want you to be doing this year? God's Word is eternal, right?

So it is—if we're talking about the Bible. But we are always changing, hopefully always growing, and God knows it. And because of that His instruction for us does too. Sometimes we're living with that expired word. It's not that God didn't say it: it's that He said it ten years ago.

In the Bible, Peter compared God's Word to milk. "As newborn babes, desire the pure milk of the word, that you may grow thereby" (1 Peter 2:2). But if you've ever cleaned out a refrigerator, you know that *milk spoils*. It doesn't last for a year, no matter how good your refrigerator is.

And here's the thing: God never intended for all His instructions to last. He might call us to work a job for several years. And when our work there is done, He might call us to another. He might ask us to volunteer twenty hours a week in one season, then move into a season of rest and regrouping to prepare us for the next big thing. But unless we're praying and paying attention—listening to God every step of the way—it can be easy to keep laboring past the expiration date.

Bread goes stale. Apples rot. Think about all those Israelites wandering around the desert after they left Egypt, receiving manna— literal food—from heaven. But that manna was good for only a day. God is eternal. His *Word*, we're told in John 1:1, was with us from the beginning. And His promises never fade and never falter—even if they might take months or years or even centuries to come to pass. But His creations are constantly changing. And so it's natural that His *instruction* may change over time too. Each season He might give us a new word. Each life change we go through might require new instruction from God. We can't just keep the old one in our spiritual fridge.

> HIS PROMISES NEVER FADE AND NEVER FALTER— EVEN IF THEY MIGHT TAKE MONTHS OR YEARS OR EVEN CENTURIES TO COME TO PASS.

The Scary Calling of God

As we talk about God's instruction and God's calling, let's be honest with ourselves. Sometimes we may be a little scared about what He might ask us to do. What if God's instruction isn't something we want? Do we even want to make God's dreams our own? What if God's dream is something that we'd deem terrifying or life-changing?

If we're honest with ourselves, sometimes we want to walk away from God's call. We try to back out of God's instruction.

Listen, I get it. It's natural. Check Scripture, and you'll find that there are a lot of spiritual giants who said no or "not yet," or at least expressed some serious reservations. Moses (Exodus 4), Gideon (Judges 6:15), Jeremiah (Jeremiah 1:6)—they were all called by God. And they all said, "Who, me? Yeah, probably not." Some of them said no so often and in so many ways that God started getting frustrated with them.

Let's take another look at Moses.

In Exodus 3 we see that Moses had been following God's instruction—one that had been in place for forty years, ever since

Moses had to run away from his posh life in Egypt. It wasn't a glamorous instruction, but he was taking care of his family. He was a shepherd working to care for his father-in-law's flock.

But that instruction was about to expire. God had heard the "groaning" of the people of Israel still in captivity in Egypt. So God showed up with a new word of instruction. From the middle of a burning bush, God told Moses exactly what He had in mind.

Moses, I want you to go back down to Egypt and take My people into a land flowing with milk and honey, God said (and I'm paraphrasing here). *I want you to talk to Pharaoh and make that happen.*

I can imagine Moses' fear and worry right then. Sure, God's will was unmistakable; burning bushes don't start talking to you every day or tell you to take off your sandals before you approach because the ground's holy. And Moses was a man of God. But if talking with God wasn't enough to terrify Moses, hearing what God wanted him to do sure was. *You want me to talk to* who? Moses must've thought to himself. *King of the most powerful nation on earth? You remember I had to run away from Pharaoh's court, right? And You want me to walk right into the palace, up to the throne, and ask Pharaoh to let six hundred thousand men just walk away? C'mon.*

Moses didn't say any of this, of course. But what he did say is what many of us might've said had we stood in his sandals. He started telling God why He absolutely, positively had the wrong man.

"No one will believe that You sent me," Moses said. So God gave him some abilities that would prove who sent him: *Toss that staff on the ground, and it'll become a snake. Stick your hand in your cloak and draw it out, and it'll look leprous. Take water from the Nile and pour it on the ground, and it'll look like blood.*

"I can't talk right," Moses said. God reassured him that he'd be just fine—that He'd be with Moses every step of the way.

"Oh Lord," Moses said. "*Please* send someone else."

And God got angry. I can almost hear Him sigh in frustration. *Okay, take along your brother, Aaron. He speaks wonderfully. You ready to go* now?

If a great guy like Moses was reluctant to go at first, we shouldn't be ashamed of our own reluctance or fear. But we've got to get over it. God not only made us but He made us for a reason. Just as Moses found, God has plans for us. And if we seek out His instruction, we must follow it once we know what it is.

That story reveals something else that I find really interesting. God didn't just use Aaron and the signs to make Moses more comfortable. He used some psychology on the shepherd too—and some plain common sense. He set Moses at ease by putting the *real* burden on His own cosmically broad shoulders. If you look carefully, God barely talked about Moses. God talked about . . . God.

Check out Exodus 3:7–12:

And the LORD said: "I have surely seen the oppression of My people who are in Egypt, and have heard their cry because of their taskmasters, for I know their sorrows. So I have come down to deliver them out of the hand of the Egyptians, and to bring them up from that land to a good and large land, to a land flowing with milk and honey, to the place of the Canaanites and the Hittites and the Amorites and the Perizzites and the Hivites and the Jebusites. Now therefore, behold, the cry of the children of Israel has come to Me, and I have also seen the oppression with which the Egyptians oppress them. Come now, therefore, and I will send you to Pharaoh that you may bring My people, the children of Israel, out of Egypt."

But Moses said to God, "Who am I that I should go to Pharaoh, and that I should bring the children of Israel out of Egypt?"

So He said, "I will certainly be with you. And this shall be a sign to you that I have sent you: When you have brought the people out of Egypt, you shall serve God on this mountain."

The Lord was telling Moses, *I am going to deliver them, I am going to bring them to a land of milk and honey, I am sending you, and I will certainly be with you.* This was God's job; Moses was just a tool. He was telling Moses not to worry, because Moses was no more responsible for this miraculous delivery than a hammer is for building a house.

And that's how it is with our instruction from God. We don't need to worry about whether we'll be successful or not, because God's in charge. It's God's reputation on the line, not mine, and not yours. And that's a lot less pressure, to know we're just following God's orders. And while we need to follow those orders the best we can, ultimately our work is about Him, not us. And when our work is done, people will remember God, not you. Not me. God.

I love that.

The devil tries to counter all that by convincing us to keep our eyes focused on ourselves. Often our work is all about who we are; our brands are all about who we're presenting ourselves to be.

Think about where we started the last chapter—we talked about how hard we work, how busy we are. We drive ourselves into the ground doing so many things. But so often all those "things" are really about one thing: ourselves. Not only what we achieve or how much we earn, but how we look. How we present ourselves on social media. How we present ourselves to our parents, or our mentees, or, especially, our kids. "I'll work eighty hours a week so I can get that PlayStation for my kids for Christmas," we'll say. We pretend that we're being selfless, but are we? Or are we just trying to be the hero on Christmas morning? Are we trying to take—even in that seemingly selfless act— the spotlight away from God and shine it on ourselves?

Listen, I understand image. I understand brand. You can't be an entertainer and not have at least some awareness of those pieces of our twenty-first-century lives. Those things—and a lot of other things we pay attention to—are important. We care about them. And I think God cares about them too. But if you're not careful, you'll put more importance on image than on the Almighty. You'll put more weight on *me* than on *He*. You'll put more effort into what you want than what God wants you to do.

What God was trying to do as He talked with Moses was remind the shepherd it wasn't about him. It was about Him—God—the great I AM. *Focus on Me*, God was telling Moses. Why? Because the more Moses saw God, the more Moses would be able to see himself. And it's the same with us. The more we lean on Him, the more we become ourselves. God created me and you and knows what we can be. He knows the possibilities we carry inside of us—the incredible gifts He's given us, the amazing skills He's planted in our souls. But for those gifts and skills to grow, we need God to water them. Tend to them. If we make those gifts about us, the crop's bound to fail—and we will too.

THE MORE WE LEAN ON HIM, THE MORE WE BECOME OURSELVES.

An idol is anything and everything that would cause you to say no to God. And so often, those idols are us. We were made in God's image. But all too often, we look at our image and say that we're our own god.

It took some doing, but Moses finally accepted his new instruction, replacing the expired one he left behind at that burning bush. He left his work as a shepherd—the place where God had sent him for forty years—and picked up his mantle as a leader. He went back to Jethro, his father-in-law, and told him he had to return to Egypt.

Moses lived about fourteen hundred years before Paul wrote his letter to the Romans. But Moses still experienced what Paul wrote about in Romans 12:1–2. He became a living sacrifice, holy and acceptable to God. He was transformed by the renewing of his mind—transformed from a mere shepherd into the leader of a great nation, the rescuer of a whole people, a man who spoke face-to-face with God Himself.

What does God have in mind for you? What are His instructions for you right now? Have you asked Him? Have you prayed about it? Fasted through it? Have you taken time to listen to Him? Tried to learn from His Word?

Or are you living according to an expired instruction? Do you believe that you've followed God faithfully, and now He's calling you to do something new? Something equally fulfilling?

Or is it possible you're scared to hear what God's plans might be?

I get it. I really do. The uncertainty. The frustration. The fear. But ask God, and you won't regret it. His instruction is waiting for you, I believe. He wants you to join His work—to be the tool in His hands to serve His purpose and to do what you were always meant to do.

To follow God's instruction can be hard—even terrifying. But I can promise you that Moses wouldn't have wished for anything less.

CHAPTER FOUR

Shift the Focus from
Stuff to Strategy

Maybe back when Moses first talked with God at that burning bush, he secretly wanted to ask Him for something else. Maybe for just a split second, Moses thought that God had come to do something for him—not the other way around. Would he have asked for more sheep? Or maybe for a return to power, like he had known in Egypt?

Here's the funny thing about that: God had other things in mind for Moses. He didn't want to make Moses more comfortable as a shepherd or prop him up on Pharaoh's throne. But when you think about it, God *did* give Moses more sheep—in the form of a million or two Hebrews looking for a new home. And God *did* give Moses power—more than Moses would've ever dreamed of. But it took time for Moses to grow into that role and learn how to use those gifts wisely. And even when Moses was following God's instruction full throttle, he made some mistakes along the way.

Sometimes I wonder what would've happened if God had immediately answered my prayer for a larger church building—given me my heart's desires right when I first asked. What if God had quickly given *me* that million-dollar donation my friend's church received? What if God had given *me* a beautiful new building when I bowed my head and asked for it? What if God had given me everything *I* thought I needed?

Easy answer: I would've squandered it all. Every blessing God gave me, I would've used unwisely. The proof? I didn't have a plan! Me trying to use God's blessings effectively would've been like a house cat trying to take down a deer, or a dog trying to use an iPhone. All the goodness that God had planned for me would've gone to waste because *I* didn't have a plan. I hadn't asked God about His plan. I wasn't prepared.

One of the biggest tragedies I can imagine is for God to take an unprepared person to a place He's prepared for them. And I think it'd be a tragedy in God's eyes too. So He prepares us. He makes us wait. He makes us stronger. He gives us the opportunity to grow *into* those prepared places. But that growth isn't always easy, or fast, or comfortable.

At Forward City, it took a while for preparation and planning to take root. My *heart* had changed with the snap of a finger. I knew right away, while sitting in that SUV, that I needed to go in a radically new direction—that I hadn't been praying for the right thing. But to see a plan take real root in the church took a little time.

Planning Pains

When I first came back from that trip to Charlotte, everyone at Forward City could see something in me had changed. And it was a shock.

I'd been startled by the revelation I'd had in Charlotte. I'd been transformed by that encounter—a real Romans 12:2 moment. I didn't need a bigger building or a larger parking lot. I didn't need more staff. I didn't need more *stuff.* I needed a strategy. I knew I needed to make substantial changes. And that meant that our church needed to make substantial changes—how we thought, how we operated, how we planned, and how we prepared.

I returned from Charlotte, full of passion, big ideas, and a disturbing amount of energy. So of course my staff was surprised.

It was a little like how you might feel if you were a kid, being raised in a family without a lot of rules: dirty dishes in the living room, unmade beds in the bedroom, filthy sinks in the bathroom. And then suddenly, Mom comes home and shouts, "Hey! We can't live this way! I'm going to clean my room right now! And you know what? You're going to clean yours right now too! And then we're going to wash the dishes and put them away! And then we're going to scrub the grout in the bathtub tile! And then we're going to—"

As a kid, you'd probably be thinking to yourself, *Whoa, hold on! Let's back up a little. Take a breath, Mom, I've got homework to do.*

I was like that mother. It wasn't that I just wanted the floors to be mopped, the closets to be cleaned, the chairs to be in perfect rows. There was that, too, but I was putting together a plan. I wanted to incorporate some planning software into the church's operations, to really get serious about thinking about how we could best use our current space, and team, to do great things for the glory of God. From Sunday morning to Saturday night, I wanted everything to be in order, given the resources we had. I was thinking about our strategy. I was remembering Luke 16:10: "Whoever can be trusted with very little can also be trusted with much, and whoever is dishonest with very little will also be dishonest with much" (NIV). I wanted to be trusted. I wanted to be a great steward of what God had given me—believing that if I did so, God would trust me with more. I just kept thinking, and saying, "We've got to do better. I refuse for our lack of preparation to delay His promise."

Change, any change, is stressful. And to some team members, this kind of massive change came as a jolt. I was asking a lot of my team all at once, and some of them weren't ready for it.

But as time went on, it became less about my micromanagement and more about my stewardship. Week after week, even as I was asking each staff member to work harder than ever before, I was pointing to the vision I had for Forward City. I kept preaching the plan. I pushed into the concept of using all the gifts and all the resources that God had given us as wisely and as efficiently as we could.

And slowly, after a few hard months, something incredible—something miraculous—happened. God's dream for us became the team's dreams. God's vision became a shared vision. The team saw what God revealed to me. They fell in love with what I believed the church could be, and more important, they fell in love with the process of getting there. Forward City became a place of life and vibrancy again—but this time we had a strategy, and we were engaged in preparing for the fulfillment of that plan. The process of planning, preparation, and stewardship became a special, fun, and exciting experience for everyone.

WE WERE ALWAYS PRAYING— PRAYING FOR GOD'S BLESSINGS, HIS INSTRUCTION. BUT WE WERE MOVING OUR FEET TOO.

There's an old African proverb that goes like this: "When you pray, move your feet." That's what we were doing. We were always praying—praying for God's blessings, His instruction. But we were moving our feet too. We were maximizing the blessings we had been given. We were following His instruction the best we could.

One day, a woman who'd been with us since the beginning—five years' worth of Forward City's changes, from its exciting opening act to its difficult period of trial to this stressful time of change—came up to me, tears in her eyes.

"Thank you," she told me. "Thank you for giving us this vision."

The church had been waiting for me. God had been waiting for me too.

It'd been a long wait. I had been like a rookie quarterback taking his lumps—learning how to lead a team in good times and bad. We'd been through seasons of stress, anger, weariness, and sadness. But now, five years after we'd first opened the doors, we were ready. It felt like we were on the right path, following the direction God had revealed to us.

Forward City was now as good as its name. Forward City was moving forward.

Joint Custody

The plan for Forward City was simple, straightforward: *maximize.* Do everything we could with everything we had. Use our talents, time, discipline, and drive to show people the love, power, and beauty of Christ. Show the city of Columbia what a loving community of Christians could be and what it could do. We wanted to do what Paul asked us to do in Ephesians 5:15–16: "Look carefully then how you walk, not as unwise but as wise, making the best use of the time, because the days are evil" (ESV).

That was our plan—our unwritten strategy. All the little details we followed were focused on that plan. Everything we did fed that plan. Every time we collected food for the hungry, every time we scrubbed a toilet, every time we stood up on stage and sang and preached and prayed, it was all for that plan. Every week I talked about it. Every day I tried to live it out. A million little details feeding into one massive goal.

In the realm of planning, be it a military operation or a business venture, you engage in two types of planning: tactical and strategic. Tactical planning is about what needs to get done that day or that week. On a battlefield, it's literally the tactics you need to use to push the forces back and win the battle. Strategic planning, meanwhile, addresses your broad, overall goals over several weeks or months or even years. Tactical planning wins battles. But strategic planning wins wars. And all those tactical decisions should feed into your overall strategy.

That's what God was showing me in North Carolina: how to think strategically. Every day-to-day, tactical decision that my team and I made for Forward City during that time fed into an overall strategy—one that God showed me in Charlotte. Everything pointed to one beautiful desire: to make the church into something that God could truly use, no matter how much money or how much space we had. And it came knowing that if we counted our pennies, the dollars would come. The tactics would feed the strategy. A thousand little details would paint the big picture.

Look at God's creation and you'll see how true that is—how little details create a huge, beautiful picture. Countless cells make up one beautiful, surprisingly complicated leaf. Countless leaves grace a majestic tree. Countless trees fill a forest. And you see it in our lives too. The average lifespan consists of more than two billion seconds, according to math.answers.com. And in God's calculus, every second can make a lifelong difference. We can choose how we'll react to an insult or how we'll respond to a child or whether to hug someone or shake their hand. It's a cliché to say that every second counts. But it's true.

IN GOD'S CALCULUS, EVERY SECOND CAN MAKE A LIFELONG DIFFERENCE.

And while you're the one who decides how you'll use those seconds, God has a plan for you as a whole.

He has a strategy in mind for your life. But for that plan to materialize, the choices you make with your seconds count. Your own strategy should go hand in hand with His—at least, if you want it to be a successful strategy.

I think there's something powerful in planning—even if that plan changes along the way. The process of planning tells God, "Hey, I'm serious. This isn't just a dream. This isn't just something I want *You* to do for *me*." When it comes to His work, God believes in joint custody.

It's worth pausing here because I don't want to be misunderstood. God has a plan for you. But if you reject His strategy? His own overall strategies—His global, universal, creation-wide strategies—will still come. God doesn't need you to do His work; God doesn't need your help to make His own plans become reality. But He *wants* it. And *you* need it.

Think about a woodworker putting together a cabinet as his five-year-old son watches. "Hand me that screwdriver," the woodworker might say. "Not the one with the flat end, but with the cross-shaped point." He might tell him that it's a Phillips screwdriver. He might say what it's used for. As the day goes on, the father could ask his boy to hammer in a nail or sand a board or help him hold two joints together.

Now remember, the kid's five years old. How much help could he be? That cabinet might be finished a lot more quickly if the expert just did the work himself. Honestly, the boy is just slowing him down.

So why doesn't the woodworker tell his son to go away? Encourage the kid to play with his toys or watch YouTube videos while the expert gets the job done?

The woodworker has three reasons to allow this unskilled assistant to "help" with the work. First, he knows that by *helping*, his son is *learning*. He's learning the difference between a flathead and a Phillips screwdriver, learning how to sand a surface, learning how to drive a nail. And while that five-year-old might slow things down now, by the time that boy is twelve he'll be far more helpful—and have a wealth of experience to tackle his own projects. That boy might even develop a lifelong love of woodworking, one that leads to a lucrative career or a rewarding hobby.

The second reason is more intangible but far more important: *The father loves his son*. His son loves his father. And so, in the midst of stacks of wood and boxes of tools, in the midst of the ringing hammers and the hiss of sandpaper over wood, that love is shown. That love grows. When that five-year-old is thirty, those moments of work with his father might be some of the most treasured times of his whole childhood. And when his *own* son is five, he might say, "Hey, you want to help me build a bookcase?"

So the woodworker asks for his son's help because (1) the son learns from the father, (2) the father and son are growing closer through this shared activity, and (3) the father simply loves spending time with his little boy. It seems so obvious, doesn't it? We're always at risk of overlooking it. The father doesn't just love his son: he loves the time they spend with each other. Every moment they spend working on that bookshelf is a moment together.

Think about the God we know from the Bible—the God who teaches us and loves us to help Him with His work.

- "Hey, Noah!" He says in Genesis 6 (and I'm paraphrasing here). "Make yourself an ark of gopherwood, and cover it inside and outside with pitch. Make it three hundred cubits long and fifty cubits wide."
- "Hey, Moses!" He says in Exodus 25. "Make a chest of acacia wood and make it two-and-a-half cubits long, a cubit-and-a-half wide, and a cubit-and-a-half high. And then cover it with pure gold."
- "Hey, Joshua!" He says in Joshua 6. "Circle the city of Jericho

with all your soldiers for six days. Have seven priests carry seven trumpets made from rams' horns."

Keep in mind, this is the God who made all of creation in six days. You don't think He could've made a boat if He wanted to? You don't think He could've brought down the walls of Jericho with just a word? This is *God* we're talking about. He can literally do *anything* He wants to do. But God brings us into the process. Why? Because He's teaching His beloved beings how to follow Him. He's teaching us how to do things right. All those instructions God gave people in the Bible were not just about bringing about something beautiful and useful and powerful. They were about building the builders too—preparing them for the blessings He hopes to give us, making them into instruments of His power and grace, shaping them into the people He intended us to be. He's not just making arks; He's making *us*.

But there's more. He wants us to participate because He's our Father. He loves us, and He enjoys showing that love through work. And when we work with God, we're showing how much we love Him too.

Moving from Dreams to Plans

I know the plans that I have for you, God tells us in Jeremiah 29:11. But something beautiful can happen when you bring your own plans to the throne, when you tell Him how you want to serve Him. He loves you. He wants to encourage you when your strategies align with His. He's your *Father*. If He's building a bookcase and you ask to help, God will rarely turn you away—unless He has another job in mind for you. And if you suggest to Him that you build a bookcase together, He'll listen. But that doesn't mean that God will always say yes. His plans and yours must—to use a woodworking term—dovetail.

I wanted to serve God through leading a church. Your plans might be different from mine. God gave you different talents and abilities and desires. You might be praying about starting a business, or a family. You might be trying to fix the family you have now or patch up half-broken relationships. You might feel an anointing to feed the hungry or educate the needy or travel halfway around the world to bring God's Word to people who've never heard of Him. Or who knows? Maybe you feel a call to get up on stage and sing about God's glory and mercy and love.

All those are admirable dreams. But they're not *plans*. Not yet. They're not enough to tell God you're ready for Him—that you're ready to work with Him. That you're ready for that joint custody.

I've been a Los Angeles Lakers fan for most of my life, and my favorite player—by far—was the late Kobe Bryant. He's considered one of the best basketball players to ever set foot on a court. Over the course of twenty years, he was an eighteen-time All-Star, twelve-time All-Defensive Player, and won five world championships. But none of that success came through dreaming. While God gifted him with some amazing physical abilities, Kobe honed those abilities through one single-minded strategy: "I wanted to be the best basketball player ever to play, and I didn't have time for anything else that was outside of that lane," he once said.[1] And he put that plan in motion when he was just thirteen years old.

His teammates said that Kobe was always the first one in the gym, even when he was in high school. One of his high school teammates, John Celestand, was kind of happy when Kobe broke his wrist during the 1999–2000 season, simply because he figured he'd finally beat Kobe into the gym in the morning. No chance. The next morning, Celestand said, "Kobe was already in a full sweat with a cast on his right arm and dribbling and shooting with his left."[2] An Olympic Team USA trainer said that Kobe once started a workout at 4:15 a.m.

He wouldn't leave until he'd made eight hundred shots—and that came at 11 a.m.[3]

For all his remarkable ability, Kobe never would've become the player he was without that dedication. Without that strategy.

And you know what? I think that's the sort of dedication God wants to see in us. After all, God gave us our talents and abilities. Wouldn't He want us to maximize those talents? Wouldn't He want us to hone our abilities as much as possible? That doesn't happen without a plan. And planning begins with this: a clear, simple outline.

Keep It Simple

A plan is not a plan if it's not *plain*. It should be simple. It should be dummy proof. Sure, details are important. But those details should revolve around one straightforward plan. Even if it's a complex plan, you should know it and understand it well enough to boil it down, simply, to anyone.

Think about your plan as being an elevator pitch. Everybody who starts a business knows they must have one. If you find yourself on the elevator with a CEO or an executive and you have a big plan, that might be the only chance you have to tell them about it. You've got twenty seconds to sell your idea so quickly that, after the elevator stops, the CEO or executive hands you their business card and tells you to call them. "Hey, let's grab some coffee," the person might say. That's the ultimate win.

You don't have the time to go into all the details. You don't want to bore the man or woman with all the complexities. The plan needs to be simple, straightforward.

That simplicity is important in an elevator speech for obvious reasons. But it's also important for you, the planner. Why? Because it keeps you focused on the plan. Details are important to your plan's success. They're critical. But if you let them drive the car, they'll take you places you don't want to go.

Ask the Pharisees about that. In Jesus' day, from what we read in the Bible, their religion started revolving around the details: You couldn't swat a fly on the Sabbath, because you'd be guilty of hunting. You couldn't spit into the dirt on the Sabbath because you'd be guilty of plowing. If your house was burning down on the Sabbath, it was a given that you couldn't put the fire out. But did you know that you couldn't even pull your clothes out of the burning building? That'd be work, of course. But if you wanted to put several layers of clothes on *before* you fled from your house, well, that'd be okay.

When Jesus came, He reminded us that it's the plan that's important: "You shall love the LORD your God with all your heart, with all your soul, and with all your mind. . . . You shall love your neighbor as yourself" (Matthew 22:37, 39). Jesus told us that on those two commandments hang the rest of the law. In other words, Jesus was saying that the details serve the plan, not the other way around.

Write It Down

Throughout Scripture, God told His servants to write down what He said or what they saw. He told Moses to write Israel's defeat of the Amalekites "for a memorial in the book and recount it in the hearing of Joshua" (Exodus 17:14). When He was about to teach Israel a very serious lesson, God commanded Isaiah to "write [the prophecy] before them on a tablet, and note it on a scroll" (Isaiah 30:8). Jesus told John to write what he saw in a book (Revelation 1:11). And in Habakkuk 2, God told the prophet to:

Write the vision
And make it plain on tablets,
That he may run who reads it.
For the vision is yet for an appointed time;
But at the end it will speak, and it will not lie.
Though it tarries, wait for it;
Because it will surely come,
It will not tarry.

—verses 2–3

There's something about taking your ideas out of thought and *actualizing* them—putting them down on paper so that they can be seen.

Of course, it obviously doesn't have to be written on paper with a No. 2 pencil (though some scientists say that writing your ideas in longhand creates muscle memory, which helps you remember what you wrote). Type it out on a computer. Dictate it into your phone. Make a video describing what you hope to do. The important thing is getting those ideas out of your heart and mind and bringing them into the world. There's something about writing things down that makes them feel more real. There's a sense of accountability that comes with that. It's not just your pie-in-the-sky dream anymore; it's out there.

Putting your prayers, dreams, and goals down on paper does a number of different things, and some are pretty obvious. First, if you write down your ideas, you're not going to forget them. There's less likelihood that those ideas will twist and warp in your brain too. Second, it helps clear brain space for other things—like thinking through how to make those ideas happen. Third, writing it down helps crystalize your thoughts.

I think of those ideas as babies. When even the best ideas are just in your brain, it's a little like the ultrasound of a baby. It's there, you can see it, but it's all fuzzy and black-and-white. Trying to make out exactly what it is can be hard. Is that its head or its leg? But when that idea makes it out of your brain and onto paper, you can see it better. *Hey, it looks like me*, you might say. That baby becomes real—not just part of an abstract black-and-white picture.

When you put a prayer request down on paper, you birth the plan, in a way. You can hold it. And that's when you can watch it grow.

But maybe the biggest benefit is simply this: Writing it down lets God know you're serious. That you know what you want to do and you're working out how to make it happen. When you've got a clear plan that people in the natural world and supernatural beings on the celestial plane can run with, that's when the resources come. I've seen it.

Gather People Who Can Make Your Strategy a Reality

People are the natural enemy of the supernatural. They can throw a wrench in your work for God. Those doubters can be like the naysayers we meet in Nehemiah, mocking and doubting the work you're trying to do for God.

Nehemiah was the governor of Judea around 444 BC, back when Persia ruled the land. It was a time when the Israelites—who'd been conquered by Babylonia and taken away from their homeland about 150 years before—had come back and were once again living in the land that God had promised them. But Jerusalem, Judea's most important city, was still pretty ruined (thanks to Babylonia), and its city walls were still torn down. Nehemiah, a Jew who had been cupbearer to the Persian king, asked if his people might rebuild those walls. "Sure," the Persian king said, and Nehemiah left for Jerusalem.

But a lot of folks didn't like the idea of those walls being rebuilt.

Sanballat, a Samaritan (a people closely related to the Jews but with whom they had a lot of bad blood), was Nehemiah's chief critic—and he did everything he could to keep those walls ruined.

They tried ridicule. "What are these feeble Jews doing?" Sanballat jeered in Nehemiah 4:2. "Will they fortify themselves? Will they offer sacrifices? Will they complete it in a day? Will they revive stones from the heaps of rubbish—stones that are burned?" But when that didn't work, they plotted violence. The threats grew so bad that workers gathering materials could use only one hand to carry them. In the other hand, they held weapons to ward off any attack (verse 17).

The world we live in is filled with Sanballats, too, and because of their own doubts or jealousies or pettiness, some will try to wreck your plans.

But Nehemiah also needed people to rebuild that wall. He needed people who were on board with his plan—and he found them.

We need to do the same. We need to find people who are going to buy into our vision. This is an area where your plan's clarity comes into play: Make it simple. Make it straightforward. And, when people see what you see, feel what you feel, they'll work alongside you to make that happen. That's not only true in building a church or making a business, by the way. It's true in mission work, in raising a family, in just living life. Whether you're by yourself in a two-room apartment or a great big house filled with lots of grandkids, you should have friends and associates who can see the world as you see it and who can help you with your goals and strategy. And you, of course, can help do the same thing for them.

Think about what Paul wrote in Philippians 2: "Therefore if there is any consolation in Christ, if any comfort of love, if any fellowship of the Spirit, if any affection and mercy, fulfill my joy by being *like-minded*, having the same love, being of one accord, of one mind. Let nothing be done through selfish ambition or conceit, but in lowliness of mind let each esteem others better than himself. Let each of you look out not only for his own interests, but also for the interests of others" (verses 1–4).

When you work with people who all share the same vision, you can do amazing things.

WHEN YOU WORK WITH PEOPLE WHO ALL SHARE THE SAME VISION, YOU CAN DO AMAZING THINGS.

But it's important to bring people aboard who not only share our vision and buy into our strategy but bring their own unique skills with them. It's not just what we have in common that makes us strong; our differences also strengthen us.

We don't need to look any further than Jesus for an example of that. He brought in disciples who shared a common goal but went about things very differently. The Peter we meet in the Bible was a bold, brash fisherman who sometimes, literally, got in over his head (Matthew 14:22–33). Matthew was a tax collector (9:9) who probably would've known his way around a modern-day spreadsheet. Thomas was best known for questioning whether Jesus came back from the dead. He told his fellow disciples, essentially, "I'll believe it when I see it" (John 20:25). But when Thomas saw, he *did* believe— and while Jesus scolded him, Thomas remained an apostle in good standing. Honestly, in life, sometimes you need to have people around you who ask the tough questions. Because you know that those outside your circle are going to be asking those very same questions.

We know that the disciples argued. We can assume they didn't all agree on everything. You think Jesus was surprised that all His disciples approached discipleship a little differently? No way. He knew *exactly* what He was doing. Jesus knew that those differences made His leadership team stronger—and that those differences would pay dividends when He was gone. The Bible and Christian tradition tell us that after Jesus left this earth, the followers that remained did some incredible things.

People come with a shared vision, but their own talents are important in almost every facet of life you can imagine. Successful businesses have all types of people involved in them—from big-dreaming visionaries to dedicated, detail-minded workers. Go online, and you'll find a ton of personality quizzes designed to shine a light on how people think and feel and (important in a business context) operate. Often companies work hard to hire and foster the right mix of people—all who share the same big strategy but fit in that strategy a little differently. I'm an optimistic, big-picture guy, so I need to have people in my circle who can keep me on schedule, fill in the details, and, sometimes, even rein me in a little!

But it's true in the home too. In good marriages, husbands and wives share the same goals—to love each other, build a life together, and, more often than not, raise good, healthy kids—but they bring different skills to the party. One might be a great cook while the other can't boil water. One can easily keep track of the kids' soccer practices and piano recitals while the other just goes where he or she is told. One might be precise and orderly, the other chaotic and fun. Put them together, and you have a powerful team leading the family.

That brings up an important point: a lot of moms and dads don't have that partner to complement them.

My mom was one of those strong, loving, single parents. For most of my childhood, she reared me and my sisters in truth and love, all while preaching and teaching and putting food on the table. I wouldn't be here, writing this book, without my mom. But to those brave, frazzled single parents, let me suggest something: Look for people in your life who can complement you. Look for good people to help mentor your kids. Parenting is perhaps the most challenging job most of us will ever have in our lifetimes. And as strong and thoughtful and wonderful as you may be, it's hard to do it alone. "Bear one another's burdens, and so fulfill the law of Christ," Paul wrote in

Galatians 6:2. If our goal is to raise healthy, happy kids, part of our strategy—especially if we're single parents—should be to find good people to help.

Don't Be Afraid to Change

This may feel like I'm overturning everything I said earlier. *Make a plan! Stick to the plan! Stay committed to the plan!* But I think we're talking about two different kinds of plans here. One plan is the vision. It's what we're trying to accomplish. It's the strategy of *what* we're trying to achieve and *why*.

But then there's the plan of the *how*. How do we fulfill that *what*? How do we satisfy that *why*? How can we follow that vision in a culture that's forever hanging?

Historically, Christians have been pretty good at staying true to the *what* and *why* while changing the *how*.

When Peter and the other disciples started spreading the word of Jesus, they were mainly talking to fellow Jews—people who knew the prophecies of a coming Messiah and were aware of Jewish law and tradition. When Paul started preaching to folks outside the Jewish faith—Gentiles who came from a very different tradition—he had to change the *how*. In Acts 17 he praised Greeks for their religiosity and referenced an altar in town dedicated to "an unknown god." He told his shocked audience that "the One whom you worship without knowing, Him I proclaim to you: God, who made the world and everything in it, since He is Lord of heaven and earth, does not dwell in temples made with hands" (verses 23–24). He didn't talk about Jesus' Jewish lineage. He didn't talk about Messianic prophecies. His audience didn't know or care about either.

Christians are often on the lookout to show God's love in the midst of world events and crises. Christian doctors fly to disease- or famine-ridden countries. Preachers talk about current events from the pulpit, emphasizing how the love of Christ can be seen and felt even in the darkest of times. Countless churches, including Forward City, respond to the specific needs of the communities they serve—giving out food and shelter and, hopefully, the love of Jesus during difficult seasons.

Think about Forward City Church. Our goal—our *plan*—is always to reach people, all the lost souls that we can possibly reach. That's the *why*. That *why*, that vision, is never going to change. The *how*? It changes all the time. It changes with what's going on in our streets. It changes with what's going on in our city. It changes with what's going on in the world. As the world pivots, so do we—all while keeping our eyes and hearts and message focused on the eternal, unchanging truth of God.

Take technology. When I was growing up, the churches that I experienced were pretty low-key when it came to technology. A lot of churches still are—and maybe, given where they're located and who they're serving and who they're trying to attract, that works for them. A thriving church doesn't *need* screens and light shows.

But Forward City does. We're a new church with a young congregation, trying to reach people who've been raised in an era of pyrotechnic concerts and TikTok. To reach a younger generation—a generation starving for God—we believe we need to speak in a language they understand, to use tools that resonate with them. If we're not equipped technologically, we may be limited in our ability to reach certain people.

I think evolution—personal evolution, cultural evolution—is a natural part of life. Pick a plant or pick a person, it doesn't matter. If you don't change and adapt and evolve, you won't make it.

We, as Christians, need to think about how we can serve God in these times too. Just as we all go through different ups and downs, so does everyone around us. So does our neighborhood. Our city. Our country. Our world. And even as important as our own needs are—the stuff that we need, the stuff that God wants us to pray for—we should always keep focused on God's strategy too. His instruction for you. His plan for the people around you.

Are you praying for the wrong thing? Are you praying for the stuff you need without thinking about God's strategy? Are you thinking about how God can serve you instead of how you can serve God?

Planning for Blessings

But it's not just businesses that need plans. It's not just churches. You need a plan for your life. You need to let God know that you're ready for *His* plans and blessings.

What is missing in your life? What do you feel that you need? What are you crying out to God for?

Back up. Rewind. Think about what you're asking for. What you're *praying* for. Push away all those longings for what you don't have and look at what you do have.

What's your strategy? What's your instruction? And what do you have to help fulfill God's instruction? What do you start with? Consider your talents and skills. Think about your work and what you do for fun. What do you love to do? What *would* you love to do? How can God use that? Take what you have and make a plan. Don't just dream about it, don't just fantasize. Write it down. Give it shape. Give it *life*. And then, ignore the Sanballats of the world and find people who want to give your vision life too.

Starting your plan doesn't need to cost a dime more than the price of a pen and paper. It'll take some time, perhaps, but it'll be time well spent.

Show God what you want to do; present your prayers to Him. Write them down—not so that He can read them but so you can. And then make these prayers—and the strategy behind them—part of your heart and soul. Let them move you and motivate you. And then watch the work be done. Watch what He does next.

CHAPTER FIVE

Favor Will Always Find the Faithful

I know what it's like to steward God's favor through tough times. I know what it's like to try to be faithful when, from the outside, people might say, "Hey, Travis! Time for you to get a real job!"

I got interested in music early—probably when I was seven or eight years old. And even way back then, it was spoken over me that I was going to have success as a musician. God would show me His favor. "Your name will be in lights," I was told.

No one told me about the pain that'd be part of the journey. No one said anything about the betrayals. None of that was spoken to me. But that music would be a part of my life? That I'd touch countless people by God's grace through His gifts? God gave me that vision of my future. God gave me that to hold on to. And I needed that vision, because it was going to be a long time before it came true.

I believed God had plans for me in the world of music. Big plans. I believed in that macro-level promise wholeheartedly. But how would it happen? I had no idea. And I had no clue that it was going to take so long. I tell people now that I was a big plane in God's plan; I needed a long runway. But before that plane took off, I went through some tough times. I never doubted God. I never stopped believing in His instruction. Still, despite my faith and despite my faithfulness, it was hard.

I graduated from Georgia Southern University in 2006 and started working for a traditional church. I was doing both youth ministry and music for them, and in a lot of ways, it was pretty rewarding—especially the youth ministry part. Before I accepted the job, I had no idea what it was like to truly minister to people, especially teens. But as youth pastors know, there's probably no harder, or more rewarding, job in ministry. If a drunken teen called me, I would leave my house to find them and get them to safety. I loved those kids. And the kids liked me too.

But while my kids might've loved me, it felt like the choir *hated* me. Keep in mind, this was a traditional church, and musically I'm not a very traditional guy. I had lots of radical ideas and had a much younger style than the church was comfortable with. I wanted contemporary music with a lot of energy. They wanted hymns. And while I understand now that hymns have their own beauty and place, I was twenty-two years old and not interested. "Hymns?" I said. "God left hymns, like, a hundred years ago!" The choir thought I was crazy. Our choir membership went from seventy people down to about ten.

Clearly, that church wasn't a great fit for me during that season. So I left for another church in Georgia—one that seemed to mesh with my style better but couldn't pay me nearly as well.

Meanwhile, I still held that vision in the back of my mind, and I worked on my own music. I recorded and released some under my own name. Faithfully, I pursued those dreams. But recording and releasing albums costs money, and I started slipping deep into debt. I remember having about a $10,000 balance on my Discover card at the time, and that $10,000 felt like a million. My name in lights? Those lights felt very far away.

A couple of years later, I received what I believed was a word from God to move to a small town in North Carolina—and entered, financially, the most difficult season of my life.

A guest speaker had come to preach at the church I was serving in Georgia—just some random White guy from North Carolina. But when he got up to preach, I felt something happen to me internally that I couldn't understand. His message wasn't random. His message was all about God's *favor*, and for me, it hit home. As a struggling gospel singer, I felt that I needed to unlock that favor. I knew God had favored me with *ability*. But to really share it with others, I needed to have more opportunity, more resources, more chances. And to do that, I needed to practice radical obedience. To pray for God to shape me. To open those floodgates of favor, I needed help. I needed to learn some more lessons. And I needed to learn how to follow God faithfully, no matter how hard it might be.

It felt like this pastor might be just the man to teach me.

I knew that God's favor was on me. I knew that He could shower radical grace on my life—open doors that I wouldn't be able to explain. But did I know how to manage that? Growing up fatherless, I feel there were management lessons that, as a man, I needed to learn from a man. My mom was great, and she did the very best job she could raising me, but I needed those tools from my dad.

And here was this preacher, holding out the tools. It moved me. Something in me said, *Hey, you need to follow him.* In him I saw the man who could teach me about favor and show me how to use it. So I prayed, packed my stuff, and followed. I didn't even really know anybody at the church besides him and a couple of his staff. I put my three-bedroom, two-bath house up for rent on Craigslist, rented a crappy little apartment, and told my mom that God was calling me to North Carolina. I was twenty-five years old, and it was the biggest leap of faith I'd ever taken.

And, financially at least, it looked like that leap took me straight off a cliff.

I worked at that pastor's church, but for next to nothing. I earned one hundred dollars a week to lead the church's band and youth worship, and that was it. I had hoped to get a little extra cash by renting out my house in Georgia, but a couple of months in, the guy stopped paying rent. I discovered that he smoked and he owned a dog—a big dog, the kind that shouldn't be inside—and the house was trashed. I couldn't rent it as it was. I didn't have the money to fix it up. With the mortgage behind in Georgia and rent due for my apartment in North Carolina, I was hopeless. One of the most embarrassing moments of my life happened when the bank foreclosed on my home.

My credit cards were completely maxed. I had next to nothing. I lived in a run-down apartment, and on my salary, I didn't really have enough to eat. The church would hold a lot of cookouts and I'd eat there. My friends would sometimes cook for me. I was able to buy an occasional Jr. Bacon Cheeseburger from Wendy's. One night, my younger godbrother and I ate grits for dinner. Just grits.

And I admit, I went hungry some nights. It was the first time in all my years that I'd been completely, utterly broke. It was about the lowest point in my life. I'm a military brat, and I'd never worried about putting food on the table. I'd never struggled financially. And I was too embarrassed to ask for help. I couldn't go back to my mom—after I told her that God had sent me to North Carolina—and ask for rent money. I couldn't tell her how bad it was. I couldn't tell anybody. It was bad. Really, really bad.

But on that $100-a-week salary, I still managed to tithe. The church would pay me, and I'd turn right around and give them $10 back. And when the church held a building campaign, I tried to save even more. I was determined to give $1,000 for that campaign—and I did it. At the time, it was the largest offering I'd ever given.

On the subject of favor, this preacher knew his stuff. I'd sit in his office. I'd go out to eat with him. I'd follow him around and ask questions: *How do I create a budget? What happens if I miss an opportunity? How do I deal with temptation?* Questions and questions and more questions. And he'd just sit with me and help me unpack it all.

I'd write it all down in notebooks. Tons of notebooks. I still have those notebooks, filled with all that wisdom. I was getting a master's degree in favor.

And even then, in that financial dungeon, I tried to remain faithful. I don't look back on that season with any regret or bitterness. It was a season of learning, of sowing, of stretching. Without it, I'm afraid I wouldn't possess the gratitude or the fortitude that I currently have. That season taught me how to make a lot happen with a little.

I have a master's degree in theology. I'm getting a PhD in organizational leadership. But that small town? That was my real education. It taught me everything: patience, endurance, compassion, empathy. I don't think I'd be a good pastor without that season. It taught me to love people who don't smell good. It taught me that you can be faithful and still not have anything, materially speaking. It's difficult to truly empathize with people unless you can relate to what they've gone through.

I went to that town looking for God's favor. And you know what? I found it. It sure didn't look like I found anything but a lot of bills. But God's favor isn't just about having a nice house or job security. In fact, God's favor can feel anything but secure. God showed me His favor in the midst of my faithfulness. He taught me the lessons that I needed to learn.

Some nights, I'd bow my head to say a prayer over a nearly empty plate—over a spoonful of grits or a greasy double cheeseburger. To some people, it

> GOD'S FAVOR CAN FEEL ANYTHING BUT SECURE. GOD SHOWED ME HIS FAVOR IN THE MIDST OF MY FAITHFULNESS.

might've looked like God had taken His favor over to the other side of town. But prayer, I'd say—that closeness to God I felt—that was favor. That was worth far, far more than a plate of filet mignon.

Finding the Favor of God in Faithfulness

It's weird, isn't it? To have traveled all the way to North Carolina to learn about favor, and for it to look to everyone else like God's favor was yanked away from me?

But looking back, that hard time was part of God's favor. It was a gift. Even though I was broke, I was wealthy. Information poured into me like coins into a bag. It goes back to Romans 12:2. My life was being transformed.

To feel God's favor, you first have to be faithful. You must pursue God with love and perseverance. You must buy into His strategy, embrace His instruction. And then, when you show your love for God and His plans for you, God will show you the favor you need for those plans.

But I should tell you right now: That favor isn't necessarily about money or cars or *stuff*. It's often much more valuable, and much more beautiful, than that.

When people talk about God's favor, they sometimes think of it as having a rich uncle who'll give them everything they've ever wanted. Point to it, pray for it, and boom! It'll be theirs. And maybe before those years in North Carolina, I used to fall into that camp a little. I was taught that as long as you do what God tells you to do, you'll have . . . well, a bunch of stuff! I had to unlearn some things about the "prosperity gospel" during that season. I was doing what God told me to do, and I had nothing.

Many people around the world struggle with poverty, with hunger, with just keeping the lights on and the kids fed. And sometimes those of us who have enough—those of us who can pay our bills and drive our cars and buy a Jr. Bacon Cheeseburger without even thinking about it—we can look at those below the poverty line and think, *Well, it's got to be their fault.* And yes, sometimes it is. But sometimes you can be obedient and faithful and still be poor. Sometimes your faith can lead you to a valley. We do our best learning in our valleys.

That season taught me how to empathize. I don't think I'd be a good pastor without it. That season taught me to love people who sit on street corners with signs. People who smell. People who fight every day to make ends meet and still find it isn't enough. There are people who obey God who have nothing. As I travel the world, I see people in Africa and Asia—people who are far more dedicated to God than I am—who have nothing. They go home to houses made of tin. They cook food over an open fire, if they even have food to cook. But they pray and sing God's praises and do amazing work for their Savior. I was humbled in North Carolina. But when I see that kind of faithfulness, I'm humbled now.

I bet if I walked up to any one of those people and asked them if they had God's favor, they'd say yes. *Oh yes.*

This chapter is all about praying for faithfulness over favor. But in a way, being faithful *is* favor. When we do what we're built to do—when we love God and follow Him, heart, mind, and soul, we feel God's favor deep inside, whether we're eating grits or filet mignon.

For me, *favor* doesn't mean cars or houses or worldly success, necessarily—even though that can be a part of it. For me, favor is God's radical grace. God sweeping you up in His whirlwind of blessing. Doors open that you can't explain. You find yourself in places and you have no idea how you got there. For one person, it may mean being carried from soul-crushing poverty to a position of influence and power, where you can use those blessings to help others. For another person, it might mean *giving up* wealth and power and donating all your time and effort to a God-honoring cause you believe in—and doing so with unflagging, unquenchable joy. Both are expressions of God's favor. When you're in God's will, you are the recipient of God's radical grace, and He's liable to give you everything you need for your assignment.

Did you catch that? He's liable to give you everything you need—*for your assignment.*

One of my favorite movie series is the *Mission: Impossible* franchise. I love it so much. Ethan Hunt—played by Tom Cruise—and his fellow agents fly all around the globe, saving the world from evil crime syndicates or two-faced spies or super assassins. And in most of those movies, wherever he goes, whether it's India or Russia or Dubai, everything Ethan needs is there—squirreled away in some secret warehouse or airport locker. Passports, currency, and weapons tumble out of duffel bags. Satellites give him all the information he needs. Masks are made on the spot.

To me, that's what God's favor is. It's not this gauzy, self-serving sense of *prosperity.* It's getting everything that's necessary for your *mission.* For *God's* mission. It's as if God has a storehouse stocked to the rafters with the resources necessary for your assignment—your own *instruction,* to use a word from the last chapter. And when you say yes to the mission for your life, those doors may open and provide you with all you need.

I believe that. The Bible tells us so. "And my God shall supply all your need according to His riches in glory by Christ Jesus," Paul wrote in Philippians 4:19. But notice that phrase: all your *need.* Sometimes, like Tom Cruise finds in *Mission: Impossible,* you may find that your needs require you to stretch those resources. Sometimes those resources might be far beyond what you expected. Other times, you might need to figure out how to scale a skyscraper in Dubai with less equipment than is ideal, for instance. But God knows your needs better than you do. And believe me, if you're on God's mission, He won't leave you hanging. As I learned in that small town, hardships and obstacles can be part of God's favor too.

Opposition . . . or Opportunity?

"Be careful what you pray for," I sometimes tell people. If you pray for patience, He may respond by giving you something that requires it. If you pray for endurance, He may respond with something to endure. But the truth is, qualities like patience and endurance carry us through all manner of experiences—and we *should* pray for them. We all need patience. We all need endurance. And just as you need to work your own muscles to get stronger, pressure and obstacles help to build spiritual muscles and strengthen your resolve. Think about 1 Timothy 4:8: "Physical training is good, but training for godliness is much better, promising benefits in this life and in the life to come" (NLT).

Resistance leads to endurance. Pain can lead to patience. It's there that we find the faithfulness we need to pursue God's favor and our dreams. It's just like Paul wrote to the Romans in one of the book's most famous passages: "And not only that, but we also glory in tribulations, knowing that tribulation produces perseverance; and perseverance, character; and character, hope. Now hope does not disappoint, because the love of God has been poured out in our hearts by the Holy Spirit who was given to us" (5:3–5).

In a way, Paul was talking about faithfulness and favor. We doggedly push through our tribulations with our eyes focused on God, trusting in His strategy and His love. We follow God faithfully in spite of all those obstacles. And what do we get in return? Perseverance. Character. Hope. Those qualities? They're worth more than a seven-figure bank account, more than a Lexus in the garage. Those qualities are *gifts*. Signs of God's favor. And when God opens His storehouse to us, those qualities help us use those other gifts more wisely.

Here's another reason to be grateful when we find ourselves facing problems or obstacles: When the Enemy feels like a sumo wrestler breathing down your neck, when you feel as if you're under attack, in some cases I think attack is *affirmation*. Attack may be, believe it or not, a sign of God's favor—or of a favor to come.

Think about the movie series *Mission: Impossible* again. Why does Ethan Hunt need all those weapons and passports and masks? Because of the opposition. He needs those resources to deal with the threat. The more resources Ethan's given, the bigger the threat he's facing. And the more support Ethan and his team receive, the harder the opposition is going to work to bring them down.

Ethan's always fighting the bad guys. And we're in the middle of a fight too. "For we do not wrestle against flesh and blood, but against principalities, against powers, against the rulers of the darkness of this age, against spiritual hosts of wickedness in the heavenly places" (Ephesians 6:12). Those principalities and powers will do whatever they can to interfere with our instruction. And the more we push into that instruction, the stronger those forces will sometimes push against us.

When you're obeying God, when you're doing something that He told you to do, heaven's going to be proud of you. But hell's going to be mad. The Enemy is going to do everything in his power and his strength to keep you from whatever task you've been given. He's going to make you want to walk away. When you're following God's instruction, expect it to be a season of resistance too.

Resistance doesn't always come straight from the Enemy, of course. As we've seen, what we interpret as opposition could be a time of trial—a part of our lives when God is hoping to teach us something. Sometimes it might just be life's circumstances or an offshoot of someone else's obstacles. And sometimes, if we're being honest, we can trace the obstacles and the resistance we're facing right back to ourselves.

Take my oldest son, Jace. When he tells me that a kid in church or at school has called him a name, I sit him down and tell him that if someone's picking on him, it sometimes means that they don't like themselves very much. I don't say that those kids are dealing with their own set of obstacles, but that could very well be true. So I tell Jace that he needs to be merciful, to show a little grace toward the kid who's mistreating him.

SOMETIMES, IF WE'RE BEING HONEST, WE CAN TRACE THE OBSTACLES AND THE RESISTANCE WE'RE FACING RIGHT BACK TO OURSELVES.

But I also ask him, "Who started it?" And honestly, nine times out of ten, *he* did. I say the same thing to my congregation: "If you have opposition, you probably started it."

What I mean by that is that the Enemy only bothers those he's threatened by. When you decided to make a plan and get focused on maximizing in your current season, you started the fight. The resistance is merely his response to your personal growth. Don't be distracted by it; be *encouraged* by it. Opposition doesn't always mean you're doing something wrong. Very often, it means just the opposite.

This doesn't mean that the hard times are your fault. We all have times in our lives when it's *not* our fault—when we're facing opposition we didn't start and can't stop. We're staring at huge problems that could knock us over and wreck our plans. And whether they're put there by something else to teach us or tempt us or terrify us, or whether they're simply part of our broken world, we must deal with them. We can't just sit there passively and hope that God will wipe away every obstacle in our path. That's not what our faith is about. It's not what God wants us to do. Following God's instruction for us—following the plans to help glorify Him—means we're going to deal with resistance. And, to say it again, resistance often means that we're on the right trail. Instruction comes with opposition; a call comes with conflict. It's not a sign that we've lost God's favor. It might be a sign we *have* God's favor. But we need to lean in with faithfulness—to use all the patience and endurance and character that that opposition itself allows to grow.

And eventually we may look at all that opposition in an entirely different way. What we thought was *opposition* suddenly looks a lot like *opportunity*.

Opportunity in Egypt

Let's go back to Joseph's story for a minute, starting in Genesis 39, and consider what we see in it. Joseph was sold into slavery and bought by a guy named Potiphar, who was "the captain of the guard." With Potiphar, Joseph must've learned all about Egypt's culture and structure. He learned how to handle a big, complicated house. I'd imagine that even when Potiphar's wife betrayed Joseph, he learned something about the duplicity found in Egypt as well.

When that betrayal sent him to Pharaoh's dungeons, Joseph encountered the hardest opposition imaginable—opposition so strong that a lot of us, if we were in Joseph's shoes, would've just given up. But in those dark, difficult dungeons, Joseph found three powerful opportunities.

First, we're told that he quickly took charge of the prison. Whatever was done down there, the Bible tells us, Joseph was the one who did it. I don't know anything about ancient Egyptian prisons, but I'm pretty sure that means that Joseph was somehow in charge of distributing water and food. Prison was a massive obstacle in itself to Joseph's dreams. But it was also another opportunity to hone Joseph's organizational and leadership skills, as well as prove to people that he could be trusted with almost any problem.

Second, he met with some powerful people who were very familiar with Pharaoh's court. The Bible tells us he talked with at least two of them—the butler and Pharaoh's baker (who also told Joseph about his dreams, and whose dreams predicted the baker's own execution). I'm pretty sure that, down there in that dungeon, they talked about more than just dreams, don't you think? The baker and butler probably told Joseph all about court life above, and Joseph—being the smart guy that he clearly was—learned a lot about Egyptian politics and, most important, about Pharaoh: who he trusted and why, what he valued and why.

And third, that very dungeon was physically close to *Pharaoh himself.* When Joseph was helping his brothers in his father's fields, he was hundreds of miles away from Egypt's power center. Now he was just feet away from the most powerful man in the known world.

All of Joseph's obstacles had indeed been opportunities—opportunities not only for Joseph, to help his own dreams come true, but for his entire family to be saved from starvation. It went something like this:

After Joseph interpreted Pharaoh's dreams of seven years of plenty and seven years of famine, Pharaoh probably slapped Joseph on the back and put him in charge of, well, almost everything. He gave Joseph his signet ring—one of the biggest signs of Pharaoh's authority. Pharaoh used that ring to seal his orders, to prove that they were his orders. That means that when Joseph was given the ring, he was given the authority to speak for, and as, the king himself. By giving that ring to Joseph, Pharaoh marked him as a man he trusted implicitly, and Joseph was put in charge of all the food in Egypt's cities. The Bible says that the grain collected was "as the sand of the sea, until he stopped counting, for it was immeasurable" (Genesis 41:49).

When the famine hit, every country and region from around the world turned to Egypt. Because of Joseph, the Egyptians had food while everyone else was going hungry, and soon all of Mesopotamia was lining up outside Egypt, hoping to buy grain. That included Joseph's brothers—the very people who sold Joseph into slavery.

The events of their reunion are pretty complicated, and you probably know them already. So let's just say here that Joseph's brothers, indeed, bowed down to Joseph—not even recognizing who he was. (Joseph was forty-four by then, with dramatic differences in how he looked and acted compared to the seventeen-year-old they'd sold into slavery.) And when Joseph's brothers *did* discover his true identity, they were terrified that he might execute them.

But Joseph did something they didn't see coming: he *forgave* them. And that forgiveness came in part because Joseph understood that their evil deed brought about a lot of good—not just in Joseph's life but in the whole known world.

"It was not you who sent me here, but God," he told his shocked brothers.

Through every obstacle, Joseph saw opportunity. Through his own dogged faithfulness, he kept seeing God's favor.

Sometimes you just need to look at all those obstacles in your life in a different way. And as you faithfully work and walk in God's favor, you can make those obstacles work in *your* favor.

Pandemic . . . Problems?

When God spoke to me in that SUV in Charlotte in 2019, I came back to Forward City on fire. I had my plan. I knew what I wanted to do. I experienced a little opposition at church because I was moving so fast, but that wasn't going to stop me. *Nothing* was going to stop me. Nothing would put the brakes on 2020 being the best year in Forward City's history.

But COVID-19 had other plans.

On March 15, 2020—about a month before Easter—the governor of South Carolina announced the closure of all public schools. By April 1, he ordered all nonessential businesses to shut their doors. And while the state never officially forced churches to close, most did—and those that didn't were required to drastically modify how they worshipped.

Think about that: Churches are about *community.* They're about worshipping God with one another. Community is critical for Christians. God *designed* us to worship Him together, "not forsaking the assembling of ourselves together, as is the manner of some, but exhorting one another, and so much the more as you see the Day approaching" (Hebrews 10:25). When Paul was traveling around the Mediterranean spreading the gospel, he wasn't just converting people; he was building churches. He knew that individually we are weak. Bring Christians together, though, and we can get through anything.

Not only that, churches depend on their communities for their survival. Attendees' tithes and offerings pay the mortgage, keep the lights on, keep the staff and their families fed. Whether the church has twenty people or two thousand, it's built around the Christians who worship there. So when COVID stripped away in-person communal gatherings, few entities were affected like local churches. Take away community from church, take away that place to gather and sing and pray and listen, and it's like putting on a baseball game without anyone on the field. Given my newfound plan and my enthusiasm to push the church to new levels of excellence—pushing to maximize everything we'd been given and reaching as many people as we could—you'd think that COVID would have been a special sort of gut punch to Forward City.

But I didn't see it like that. I told my team, "Hey, this isn't an obstacle. This is an opportunity." And I believed it. I still had a mission. I still was determined to follow God—and for the church to follow God—faithfully. It wouldn't be easy, maybe. I believed God had given us the resources to succeed, even in this challenging time.

Why? Two reasons. First, everybody was shocked by COVID—except God. It didn't come as a surprise to Him. And second, the fact that He wasn't shocked by it meant that He had a plan for it. A strategy. God didn't just look at our calendar, take a Sharpie, and cross out the whole year. He didn't say, "You know, let's just wipe out 2020." God could still work through global pandemics and lockdown orders and masks. And so could we.

I bet you can think of a similar situation in your own life. It might not be keeping a church afloat during COVID. But keeping your family together, and keeping them alive and sane? That was a challenge for many during that time. Making sure your kids went to "school," even if they were traveling no farther with their laptop than the living room? Going to Zoom meetings in your kitchen?

Maybe it wasn't COVID that sent your life into a tailspin. Maybe it was the loss of a job, a change in a relationship, a crisis in your family. Maybe it was something else entirely. We all face huge challenges in our lives, and like flat tires or leaks in your bathroom, they never come on a schedule. We must adjust. We must move forward, even if we have to leap over walls and slide through gaps to do it. Challenges can force us all into what can seem like impossible missions.

But those impossible missions become possible by following God faithfully. We find we have the resources to come out safely on the other side.

I still wanted to reach people. I still had a purpose. I still had a *plan.* That plan—that strategy—didn't change. But how we manifested that plan *had* to change. And so it did.

Back then, we were still in our old building—a warehouse about the size of our current youth room. Nine hundred people were packing three services, and sometimes we were getting citations from the fire marshal, telling us we had too many people inside. So we were at our max—bursting at our spiritual seams. Organizationally, we were a mess too. Our systems were flawed. Our processes were weak. For our church, COVID wasn't a catastrophe. For us it was almost a gift—a reprieve. It was a chance for us all to catch our breath and move forward.

But COVID made doing church as we'd been doing it impossible. People weren't going to work. They weren't shopping unless they absolutely had to. How was Forward City going to move forward when we couldn't leave home? How could we open ourselves to new possibilities when we couldn't open our doors? How could a church be a church without being *at* church?

And what about our staff—the folks who made church possible?

We knew that church was about community. Jesus talked about gathering together. But COVID came around in an age when people could gather together online and still be thousands of miles away. In a digital space, friendships could grow without friends ever meeting each other in person. Why couldn't church operate the same way? What if we took our online presence and grew it too?

We didn't want to let anybody go during the pandemic, so everybody had to become a virtual employee. I told them to bring value to the church virtually—whatever that might look like. I wanted them to figure that part out. *Everybody* was doing *everything*, it seemed. And through that process, we uncovered that many of our team members had gifts that none of us had known about. For example, our church drummer did a fantastic job on stage for us, but during COVID we learned he's even better behind a camera. He's now our primary videographer. Everywhere I turned, people who had been doing one job were doing something else—and doing it well. It was an exciting time.

At first we tried not to let COVID change much. Sure, maybe no one could come to church. So we'd just take church to them! We tried replicating that church experience as much as we could—just like thousands of other churches were doing. The pattern of worship didn't change. We were still engaging in worship at that same high-decibel level we always had. I was preaching in that same charismatic manner I'd always done. We wanted to give our people a real church service, just like they were used to in person.

But then one day, as I was praying, a thought came to me: When we were doing church in person, our sanctuary could feel more like a concert, with people standing up and singing and bouncing to the music. I'd march up and down the stage when I preached, shouting and exhorting and leaning into every charismatic fiber in my body. ("High five your neighbor! Give me an *amen!*") But during my prayer time, the Lord was like, *Hey, Travis, you know what? No one's standing up at home.*

And, of course, that was absolutely right. I started thinking about how I was watching church services. Was I dressing for church? Was I standing up and clapping with the music? C'mon, man. Our family was watching services in our PJs while eating cereal. And if that's how *I* was engaging online, I could almost guarantee that's what most of our people were doing too. They were watching our services in bed. Or on the couch. They were pulling up a laptop and watching at the breakfast table.

So I figured, *If people are watching from home, why don't we do church from home too?*

It was still a production. We'd have ten people in our house at a time, making the online church service happen. Jackie and I told our neighbors we'd be filming there, so if they saw a few unfamiliar cars, they didn't need to worry. We moved couches out of the living room and moved band equipment in. We still did church. But our plan adjusted to the circumstances. The overall mission was the same, but how we *did* the mission flipped on the fly. We were following God faithfully, even though it looked and sounded and felt different. And we found that we had the resources—the favor—to do what God was calling us to do.

Instead of preaching to a room with hundreds of people in it, I taught five or six people in my living room as they took notes. I wasn't preaching as much as I was *talking*. It was a massive change for me, shifting that approach. But I had to make that change, because that house environment just didn't lend itself to my public preaching style. It was as if Jackie and I were inviting our whole church into our home. It gave the services a level of intimacy and even individuality that we just couldn't achieve in a crowded, bustling, bursting-at-the-seams building.

We tried to do the same thing for our kids' church. We did the curriculum as well as we could, of course. We had a very creative woman engaging kids through screens—thinking of little games and activities that the children could do at home. On Thursdays, we launched something we called Engaged Night. We did it on Zoom, and we encouraged whole families to sit down and join us. It helped us meet church members we'd never been able to talk with before, and it allowed them to get a little personal face time with us. We would conduct mini scavenger hunts for the families: how quickly could they find, say, a book, a pair of scissors, and a coffee mug and bring them back to the screen? And then we'd give away prizes or gift certificates to the winners. Sometimes we had themes for these Engaged Nights. We'd turn it into a 1970s-themed meeting, where you had to wear bell-bottoms or tie-dye shirts. Or maybe we'd ask participants to wear their ugly Christmas sweaters. Anything we could do to help people have a little fun and bring them together.

People were isolated. They were hurting. Some were scared. I really wanted to make sure people felt a sense of belonging. If church is about community, we wanted to give people that community on screen in really special, unique ways—leaning into what those screens allowed us to do. It was new and creative and fresh.

> **WE BELIEVE OUR FAITHFULNESS LED TO GOD'S FAVOR. GOD—AS GOOD AS HIS WORD—PROVIDED EVERYTHING WE NEEDED, AND MORE, FOR OUR MISSION.**

Here's the crazy thing: Those online services, and the way we engaged with people, turned us into a global church. Every weekend, we now have worshippers from across the country and around the world streaming our services. They might be in Florida or New York, Jamaica or Africa. And yet they look at Forward City as *their church*. I think about 45 percent of our giving comes out of the state of South Carolina now. And if that wasn't enough, we've had several dozen people who connected to Forward City online and then decided to move to Columbia. Just because they wanted to go to church here. We believe our faithfulness led to God's favor. Doors we never expected to open swung wide. We were reaching people we never would've even known otherwise. God—as good as His word—provided everything we needed, and more, for our mission.

What About You?

Look at your own life. What obstacles are you dealing with? What sumo wrestlers are pounding at your door? Are you having trouble seeing God's favor in your life?

The answer isn't to give up. Follow God faithfully. Pray to give more *to* Him, not to get more *from* Him. Pray for God's mission for your life. And if you choose to accept that mission, believe that God will give you favor and the resources to see it through. Pray for the strength to deal with obstacles. Pray for the patience, and endurance, to deal with them. And most important, pray for the creativity to see those obstacles as opportunities! Because that might be just how God sees them too.

CHAPTER SIX

Pray for the *Right* People

Of all the valleys I have walked through, of all the disappointments I've suffered, people have left the biggest scars in my life.

I believe it's the same for almost everyone. We can lose our jobs. We can suffer financial cataclysms. We can be rocked by storms, both literal and metaphorical, and we can weather them all. But nothing can wound like a friend.

This pain has been particularly hard as a pastor.

I've told you that, before I had my revelation in Charlotte, Forward City was struggling. From the outside, we looked strong and healthy and vibrant. People were coming to church. People were getting saved. We were making a difference in the city. But inside, the church was full of dysfunction and disagreement. And even as our attendance grew, our leaders were leaving. We were growing and shrinking at the same time. We were winning souls but losing staff—staff that had been with us from the very beginning. People who had joined Jackie and me on this crazy dream and said they'd be with us till the end.

Here's the other thing I've learned in pastoring: No one leaves alone. No one's content to sneak out the back door. They'll try to take other people with them—so they can feel validated when they leave. Maybe it's because they've misinterpreted something you've said or taken it out of context. They might be critical of your leadership. And let's be honest, sometimes pastors make mistakes—they do or say things they shouldn't. But whatever the cause, the rift is there. And so the whispers start. The factions take shape. Parishioners or staff either trickle out or rush out the doors in a flood. Even when they're gone, they still try to hurt you. You hear those whispers. You feel the knife in your stomach.

Social media can make it personal. I've seen posts by former members that have hurt me. They might not have mentioned me by name, but I knew they were talking about me and something I said—or something they *thought* I said. It hurt.

But then the calendar tells you, "Sunday's coming!" and you have to move on. You have to get up on Sunday and preach the gospel. You need to sing and share the Word. You need to get up on that stage and lead people, not bleed on people. And how do you do that? *Prayer.* Only supernatural help can heal that kind of hurt. You lay it all at the feet of the Holy Spirit. You pray for peace. You pray for perspective. You even pray, if you can, for the *people who left you*. People can let you down. But prayer? It never will. Sure, it can be frustrating when your prayers aren't answered or are delayed. It can take a lot of time to find that peace and perspective you ask for. I understand that. Boy, do I understand. But always remember that when you pray, you're talking to the One who will never leave you. *Never.* If everyone walks out your front door, God's still in the kitchen—eager to talk, to listen, to teach, to help.

Not everyone leaves in a huff, of course. Sometimes people just leave. Maybe they move. Maybe they find a better fit in the church across town. Sometimes members of our staff move on because they get new opportunities or find higher pay or simply feel like God is calling them somewhere else. Their instruction was to be at Forward City for a season, but now they're getting new instruction. And who am I to stand in the way?

Still, it's hard for me to watch people go. It was especially hard in that rocky season at Forward City. I'm a hoarder of people. I get really used to a relationship being a certain way, and when that shifts—no matter why it shifted or how—it's hard for me not to take it personally.

But I'm not alone. Every pastor knows what I'm talking about. Honestly, every *person* knows what I'm talking about. People leave us.

The Bible tells us that change is a part of life. The world has its seasons (Ecclesiastes 3:1–8) and so do we. The God we worship is eternal and unchanging, but everything else in our lives is in a constant state of flux. We grow, literally and spiritually. We graduate. We move. We get new jobs. We develop new interests. And not everybody we meet along our ever-changing journey stays with us for the entire ride—even if they tell us they will. See, they're changing too.

I think it's important to understand another really critical component: Just as God's foolishness is better than man's wisdom, His math is a little quirky too. Sometimes He adds through subtraction. Sometimes the Lord brings people into your life for a season and then, when that season's over, they leave. It might be painful, but often it's necessary.

> THE GOD WE WORSHIP IS ETERNAL AND UNCHANGING, BUT EVERYTHING ELSE IN OUR LIVES IS IN A CONSTANT STATE OF FLUX.

Tight Spaces

In Judges 6 the Israelites wished the Midianites *would* leave.

The Midianites were nomads "most likely living east of the Gulf of Aqaba."[1] But for about seven years, Israel was like their home away from home. Every time the Israelites would plant their crops, here would come the Midianites and the Amalekites and all sorts of other people, "as numerous as locusts" (verse 5), to ruin all the crops. Between the people and the camels who came "without number," they destroyed the land and left "no sustenance for Israel, neither sheep nor ox nor donkey" (verse 4). The whole country was starving to death because of a huge bunch of bullies.

This went on for seven years! The children of Israel essentially spent those years in hiding, even in their own lands. What could the Israelites do? They didn't have an army they could turn to, no inspiring leader to follow. They were weak. And all the neighborhood bullies took advantage of that.

In this chapter—one that delves into the importance of people and the role they play in our prayers—it's important to note a couple of things:

1. THE NATION OF ISRAEL WAS ALONE AT THIS TIME. They'd forgotten their God and were surrounded by enemies. They were separated even from each other—hiding in the mountains, cowering in caves. I'd imagine that the Israelites didn't make the best of neighbors to each other either. In their fear they thought only about themselves. They protected their own grain, safeguarded their own livestock.

2. THEY DID WHAT THEY THOUGHT WAS RIGHT, BUT IT WAS WRONG. It's pretty interesting that in the book of Judges the same phrase is repeated again and again: "In those days there was no king in Israel; everyone did what was right in his own eyes" (e.g., Judges 21:25). And so often what they thought was right was self-centered. They worshipped the wrong gods and valued the wrong things, and this led them the wrong way.

It's kind of what happens to us sometimes, isn't it? We have so many gods in this culture calling for our worship. Big bank accounts.

That corner office. That new house. That new relationship. We can turn almost anything into a god—sometimes without even knowing that we are. Even wonderful things can become gods or idols to us—from food to family to even our dedication to church. We do what's right in our own eyes. Sometimes it looks right to other people too—and yet it can still be pulling us away from God. And you and me, we're prone to the same temptations and dangers those ancient Israelites were. Maybe more.

Enter Gideon—maybe one of the Bible's most improbable heroes.

The story of Gideon, like most of the other biblical narratives we talk about in this book, illustrates many of the points I'm seeking to make. His story is about managing what you have. It's about using good strategy. It's about being faithful in really difficult circumstances.

I'll tell you how the story connects to those lessons. See, when someone follows God and God uses them, their whole life *naturally* connects to all of those lessons. But Gideon's story *especially* illustrates the importance of people—and specifically, bringing together the right kinds of people.

The first time the Bible mentions Gideon, we find him in a winepress threshing wheat. Now, that in itself is pretty weird, right? Threshing wheat was typically done outside. Why? Because you need space, and you need wind. When you thresh wheat, you beat the stalks on the ground or on something hard, which helps separate the wheat grain from the chaff (the straw and other inedible gunk). Then, in the winnowing process, you toss the grain into the air. The breeze blows away the chaff, while the good, edible wheat falls back into whatever you were using to throw it.

In fact, if you wanted to design a terrible place to thresh wheat, that design might look a little like a winepress. Back in Gideon's day winepresses were small, tight spaces—pits chiseled straight out of surrounding rock or even hammered out completely underground.

Winepresses were good for only two things: pressing the juice out of grapes to make wine and *hiding*.

That's what Gideon was doing in that winepress: hiding. He was a man of fear. And he was alone. Utterly alone.

Yet God was using Gideon's own fear to teach him something. Gideon was learning how to operate in a tight space. He was learning that, while threshing wheat in a winepress isn't easy or ideal, it could be done. He had very little room. I imagine he could barely breathe because of all the grain and chaff that were in there—floating in the air and getting into his lungs. But you know what? He was making it work. He was learning. He was developing new skills, creating new strategies for how to simply survive. And through Gideon's story—and through his fear and isolation—God is teaching us something important too.

A lot of us have been forced into tight spaces like Gideon was. Our resources are tight. Our finances are tight. Our environments are tight. Even our families—with all the responsibilities they come with—can restrict our lives. Those appointments and recitals and commitments—they can all tighten our *time*. Our opportunities are painfully limited. We struggle and push against our limits, but we can't escape them.

Isn't it possible that God's teaching you something in those tight spaces? Couldn't He be training you to deal with those very limitations—to know how to maximize what you've been given, to make your circumstances work for you, even when the world outside is filled with forces that seem bent on destroying you? These are opportunities, my friend. Opportunities.

This winepress? The Midianites thundering all around the promised land? These were obstacles in Gideon's life, to be sure. But as we'll see, they represented opportunity too.

Suddenly Gideon's threshing was interrupted by an angel. "The Lord is with you, mighty man of valor!" the angel said to him.

You don't think of angels as getting sarcastic very often, but that's the way it had to feel to Gideon. I mean, he was hiding in a winepress! Midianites were running wild on his land! *A mighty man of valor?* I imagine that Gideon laughed.

"No, Lord, there's nothing mighty about me," he essentially said. "First of all, I come from the weakest tribe [the Abiezrites, part of the tribe of Manasseh]! I come from the weakest family! And you know what else? *I'm* weak too—the least in my father's house! We're a feeble people!"

But the angel wasn't being sarcastic at all. He was dead serious. In fact, he told Gideon that God would be with him and that he would "defeat the Midianites as one man."

Then God told Gideon to do something *truly* terrifying. He told the guy to go to his father's house and destroy all the false gods there.

At this period of time, as I mentioned, the promised land wasn't a land dedicated to the Lord and filled with those who loved Him. It had become a land of *many* gods (a big reason God let the Midianites have such sway over the land in the first place). Many of the Israelites happily worshipped the Lord alongside the gods of the Canaanites (the folks who had lived in Israel before the Israelites got there). Baal was a big deal, of course. Asherah, a Canaanite fertility goddess, was another. And apparently an altar dedicated to Baal and an Asherah pole were planted right on the family property.

God wanted Gideon to destroy the altar, chop down the pole, and build a new altar—this time dedicated to Him, the *true* God. And He wanted Gideon to sacrifice a bull and burn it on the altar—using as fuel the very wood that had made up those false gods. To his credit, Gideon did as he was told. But the Bible tells us that he and ten men did it at *night* so no one would see them do it. He was still that man of fear. He was terrified of what those Baal worshippers, including his own father, would do if they found out.

The next morning, they found out.

And let me tell you, the townspeople were *furious*. They wanted to kill Gideon on the spot. But Joash, Gideon's dad, ran out and said, "Hey, don't murder him!" And while it's not in the Bible, I'm pretty sure that Joash tried to calm everyone down by telling the angry idol worshippers that, hey, maybe his son was a little soft in the head. Maybe overly enthusiastic. *Let's just all calm down*, he might've said. But then Joash did something pretty interesting.

"Listen, do you *really* want to plead for Baal?" Joash said. "Defend his honor? If he really *is* a god, Baal can speak for himself! Let him defend his *own* altar!"

Remember, the altar was on *Joash's* land. The bull Gideon sacrificed to God was *Joash's* bull. But Gideon's "crazy" stunt must've sparked something in his father too. Maybe Gideon's act reminded Joash of who he truly should be worshipping. It's almost as if Gideon was sounding a wake-up call to Joash and maybe everyone else in town.

But we barely have time to catch our breath, because the action immediately shifts back to the Midianites and the Amalekites, who were camping in the Valley of Jezreel—probably stomping all over and destroying a lot of crops as they camped.

I love this part of the story. The Bible tells us that Gideon had changed drastically too. His own "crazy" act had turned him from a man of fear to the man the angel had claimed he was—a *mighty man of valor*. He was ready to follow God's instruction.

And here's the real crazy part: about 32,000 men showed up, ready to follow *him*.

Trumpeting God's Greatness

You can imagine what happened between the time Gideon tore down Baal's altar and the time he blew that trumpet. Folks from all around heard about Joash's crazy kid. That act—which seemed so insane at the time—was the very act that put Gideon on the map. Everyone knew who the kid was. A good 32,000 people were ready to follow Gideon, not in spite of that insane act but *because* of it. Remember that just a handful of verses back, Gideon was threshing wheat in a winepress *alone*. He called himself a weak man from a weak tribe. And now he was a leader of thousands, getting ready to kick some Midianite butt.

Amazing what following God's instruction will do. It will not only change you into the person you can be but impact those around you.

Sometimes God gives us a radical instruction too. He tells us to do something that looks a little crazy. It probably won't get us killed, but it might be embarrassing or challenging. He might call you to talk with a total stranger. Or give more to your church than you feel you can afford. Or even quit your job and pursue something else. Hey, I had plenty of people who thought my own call was crazy. *Travis, you want to sing gospel for a living? That's not realistic. That's not going to pay the bills.*

> AMAZING WHAT FOLLOWING GOD'S INSTRUCTION WILL DO. IT WILL NOT ONLY CHANGE YOU INTO THE PERSON YOU CAN BE BUT IMPACT THOSE AROUND YOU.

But God loves for us to be a little crazy—as long as we're crazy for Him.

Let's flash back for a minute to pre-trumpet-blowing Gideon—the fearful Gideon threshing wheat. When the angel spoke to him, Gideon didn't just complain about how weak he was. He let the angel have it—demanding to know where God had been all this time while the Midianites were trampling all over the Israelites' land.

"Hey, if the Lord is really with us," Gideon said, "why then has all this happened to us? Why do the Midianites treat us like dirt and destroy all our grain? Where are all His miracles that our fathers told us about?"

For years Gideon had been praying for miracles that never

happened—just as we sometimes do. He had thought that he and his people had lost God's favor—just as we sometimes think we have.

But look at what was happening in Gideon's life. Maybe Joash's son didn't get the miracle that he was hoping for—not in the form he was expecting anyway. But working with the wheat down in that winepress? He'd learned to *manage* his circumstances, to maximize what he did have. He felt that he'd fallen out of God's favor. But his tearing down Baal's altar tells us that he was still living in *faithfulness*. God's warehouse for Gideon was brimming with blessings—but not in the way that Gideon would ever expect.

And now, as 32,000 men crowded into Gideon's village, ready to fight, Gideon was about to learn another crazy lesson.

Power of the People

The Bible talks a lot about how important people are. But they also have to be the *right* people. And to find the right people, you need a good process.

I wonder what Gideon thought when he and his 32,000 men camped by the well of Herod and looked at the Midianite army arrayed against him. "As numerous as locusts," the Bible says they were in Judges 7:12; "and their camels were without number, as the sand by the seashore in multitude." Later we learn that there were around 120,000 Midianites and Amalekites down there—nearly four times the number of men who were with Gideon. And while Gideon probably couldn't count them all, he could see the Israelites were outnumbered. Did he think to himself, *We don't have enough people?*

You know what God said? *You have too many.*

Think about it: You're facing a life-or-death struggle and you're already outnumbered by a huge amount, and God tells you that you've got too many men. But Gideon was trusting God fully now, walking in faithfulness. So when God told him to ask the men if they were scared, he did just that. Maybe with a few little butterflies in his stomach, he called out to his men.

"Hey! Are any of you frightened?"

A huge rumble went up from his army—whispers and low talking, maybe even a little nervous laughter.

"Whoever is fearful and afraid, leave!" Gideon told them. "Let him turn and depart at once!"

And 22,000 men did just that.

Now, 22,000 men? That's a *lot*. Think about an NBA stadium—Los Angeles's Crypto.com Arena, the Wells Fargo Center in Philadelphia, whatever arena is nearest you. You couldn't cram 22,000 people into *any* of them. Chicago's United Center is the biggest NBA arena in North America, and it seats less than 21,000. So essentially, Gideon was telling that size crowd—*plus a thousand more*—to just go home. *Don't worry yourselves*, Gideon told them. *We've got this.*

That seems insane.

In war, having *more* people is always better than having fewer . . . right?

Unless those people are terrified of fighting, of course. Unless those people would be so scared that they'd drop their swords and slings and run away as soon as the Midianites started coming toward them—sun glinting off their helmets, swords raised in the air, their voices sounding like an inhuman roar.

Imagine if those people had gone into battle. Imagine what might've happened if Gideon had expected them to not just fight but die if need be. Better to find out before the fighting started. Better to find out before the blood started to run. Better to know who to count on before it counted. As I like to say, the only thing worse than no help is the wrong help.

Gideon learned something we could all learn, especially in this age of social media, where we're all encouraged to stuff our profiles full of "friends" and where likes and shares are, for some of us, more precious than gold. We may be surrounded by people that we call friends. People we think will help us when we need them. Our lives can be filled with breakfast meetings and prayer groups and exercise classes full of folks we might like to hang out with and share a laugh or two with.

But when that laughter turns to tears, who'll still be there? Who won't be afraid?

You learn who your friends are not on the Saturday nights of this life but on the Monday mornings. You learn who your friends are not in times of joy but in times of grief and sickness and heartbreak.

How do we find out?

We pray, of course. We pray that God will send the right people into our lives at just the right times. It's amazing how often that happens, isn't it? I bet you can think about situations when a friend entered your life just when you needed a friend like her. Or your son found a teacher that sparked his love of a subject. We pray that God will send us the people we need when we need them.

But I think back to that African proverb I mentioned earlier. "When you pray, move your feet." As we talk to God, we talk with those people who come into our lives too. Sometimes it's as easy as asking them, just like Gideon did. Ask them how committed they are to what God's instructing you to do. Ask them how committed they are to the work ahead or the task before you. Ask them how much they believe in you and the relationship you have with them—be it personal or business or spiritual or what have you—and chances are, they'll tell you. Listen to what they say.

Let's just use me for an example. I'm not a fighter. If someone asks me if I'll stand with them in a dark alley when a couple of guys jump out of nowhere, I'll be honest: *not on your life*. I'm not getting into fights for you. I'm not going to get punched in the face for anybody. I'm a runner, not a fighter, and if you start a fight with somebody, I'm not going to have your back. If I was with Gideon back in the day, I might be one of those 22,000. "Hey, good luck, Gideon!" I'd say. "I'll see you back at home."

It's the same in people's lives, man. *Believe* them. I believe that, most often, people will tell you how much they can and are willing to commit. And if they're not all in? It's no crime. Just wish them well.

It's trickier to deal with those who say they are all in. People may say they'll be there for you. They may even mean it. But then the time comes to go into battle and you discover they weren't as committed as you—and they—thought.

That truth has been one of the hardest things about my journey as a pastor. At any moment, people can walk out of your life. "Yep, bye," they'll say, and you have to smile and honor them and send them on their way. I've had to grow up a lot in the past few years, because I've felt that pain often. A wise woman once told me, "While pastoring, you have to be married to people who have the option of dating you." What a brilliant quote. I immediately knew what she meant.

But I don't think that my experience is strange or unusual. Most of us—perhaps all of us—have people who walk out of our lives. They might be friends or coworkers. More damaging is when it's a parent, child, spouse, or sibling. People get scared. People get afraid of getting hurt. And sometimes people just . . . leave. They might be afraid because of their own trauma. They might be afraid because it's not their calling. It's not necessarily because they're bad people; in fact, that's rarely the case. You don't hear Gideon getting angry at the people who left. That was, very simply and very literally, not their battle to fight.

Sure, that's easier to write than to live out. It's impossible not to feel abandoned. It's impossible not to feel betrayed. And honestly, it is flat-out impossible not to grow bitter and angry toward those people without the grace of God. But we *do* have God's grace. We *can* move forward. And often, after the wreckage is cleared away and we've patched ourselves up, we look back and say that it was *better* that they left. Because where we were going, they couldn't have gone anyway.

More, Gideon discovered, isn't always better. You need people you can depend on, people who won't take off when things grow difficult. Because—and this is the truth—things always grow difficult.

Long Odds

Now, with 22,000 fighting men gone, Gideon's forces were outnumbered 12 to 1. The odds of victory were astronomically slim. But Gideon's instructions hadn't changed. God knew the limitations Gideon would be facing. In fact, He was about to saddle Gideon with more.

You still have too many people, God said. And He told Gideon to take them down to the water—probably a nearby stream. *Whoever drinks water from the cup of their hands is qualified to fight in the battle. But anyone who puts their face in the water and laps it up like a dog, send them home.* Gideon—walking in faith and listening faithfully—did as he was asked. And of those 10,000 men, 9,700 of them put their heads in the water. Only 300 drank from the cup of their hands (Judges 7:4–6).

So Gideon sent 9,700 men home.

But now, with the departure of another 9,700 men, Gideon had one man for every 400 Midianites. He was facing down an army of 120,000 people with just 300. Outside of Hollywood, those sorts of odds aren't just long; they're *insane.*

But let's look a little closer at this story.

Why did God want Gideon to send away the 9,700 men who drank like dogs? Sure, it was partly to make sure (according to the Bible) that Israel wouldn't mistake the victory as something they did instead of something He did. God wanted to make sure Gideon's people knew that He was real, He loved them, and He could do anything for them. But there was something else at work too.

The men who drank with their heads in the stream weren't worrying about anything but their own thirst. They were preoccupied with their own appetites. Their eyes were inherently down, looking at the water. And if an enemy soldier snuck behind them? It'd be over for them. One quick swing of a sword, and their stream-drinking days would've been behind them.

But the men who drank from their hands? Their eyes were on the horizon. They could look for both dangers and opportunities. They could see the Midianites in the distance. They could see their friends and fellow fighters nearby. They were *prepared.*

God was telling Gideon that he shouldn't take anybody into battle whose sole focus was on what was below them. Gideon needed men who could focus on what was *around* them. His men needed to be aware.

I love this story because it reminds me to concentrate on God, not on myself. It reminds me to focus on what I *really* need, not what I sometimes *think* I need. I don't require more. I require exactly what God says I do. I need only the help that God wants me to have. And that help God gives me? God will prepare them. He will qualify them.

Likewise, God is telling you that fearful people can't go where He's sending you. He's telling you that lack of awareness won't cut it where you're going. You need people who are brave, who are aware, who can fill the needs that God knows are present.

Obviously that has a lot of relevance for me as a pastor. Like Gideon, I literally need people in our church to help me do God's work. And there's a big reason that story is so powerful for me personally.

But it's not just pastors and CEOs and leaders that can take something away from Gideon's story. We all need good people around us. We all could use some help now and then, and that help often comes from reliable family members. Good friends. Pastors. Teachers. Neighbors. In a way, that's a big part of what *church*—not as in a building or formal community, but church as in our family of fellow believers—is all about. It's about the support we can give one another. We come together in love. We come together to help each other through the hardest times in our lives.

Looking for good people in your life? You might already know them. They might sing a little off-key. But they drink from their hands, eyes up. You'll need people, good people, to help you fulfill God's purpose. You may not be a pastor or a supervisor, but you're still called to be a leader, in your home or family or circle of friends. And if nothing else, you're leading your own life. You're a Gideon. And you could use some good, smart people in your life.

But when I read this passage, I see that it's not just about leading. It's also about following.

The Lord wanted a certain type of person on Gideon's team. He told Gideon what to look for: people who would keep an eye out for threats, who would be able to spot trouble when they saw it. Just as God called Gideon, God was calling those three hundred people to Gideon's side—giving them a holy assignment, a sacred instruction.

We focus so often on the people who leave us. We're always the Gideons in our own story, right? But sometimes we can be the holy soldiers in someone else's story. In fact, I'd say that happens a lot in our lives.

"Sociologists tell us the most introverted of people will influence 10,000 others in an average lifetime," author Tim Elmore told *Forbes* in 2017.[2] People with a big platform might influence thousands, or *millions*, more. And we can have a *huge* influence on the people closest to us: our friends, our families, our coworkers, our neighbors. Are we paying attention to that influence? I think God asks us all to drink with our hands—to keep our eyes open for opportunities and threats. To impact the people around us in a way that God would like. To laugh with them, cry with them, instruct them, even fight alongside them if need be.

As a pastor and a leader, I can easily see myself as Gideon. But you know who I am for the thousands of people I speak to each Sunday, or the millions of people who listen to my music? You know who I want to be? A guy who's trying to help them fulfill *their* holy mission—to find their instruction, to help them discern God's will for them and to pray accordingly. I'm not a leading man in their stories. I'm just a character actor who, hopefully, says something important at just the right time. A guy who sings a song that might be encouraging to someone. I'm one of the guys who wants to be drinking with his hands—looking for opportunities to help.

Where are your opportunities? Who can you help? Yes, God has some Gideon-like plans for you—to serve Him in a mighty way. But He has plans for your friends too. Your neighbors. Your children. The person standing next to you in the elevator. God calls us to care for each other. To speak a good word. Sometimes that's our *instruction*—to help someone fulfill their own instructions. Take a tip from Gideon's three hundred. Watch. Don't get scared and run away when things get tough for a friend. Don't just bend down and drink up what you need. Keep your eyes open. Watch your own horizon for opportunities to come to someone's rescue. Keep an eye on your surroundings. Seize the chance to help when you can. You'll influence so many people in your life; make sure that you're a good influence.

> SOMETIMES THAT'S OUR *INSTRUCTION*— TO HELP SOMEONE FULFILL THEIR OWN INSTRUCTIONS.

Finding the Right People

As you probably already know—or at least suspected—Gideon and his three hundred men got the job done. He split his tiny force into three even tinier ones. He handed each of them not a sword but a trumpet. And instead of handing each a shield, he gave each a clay pitcher with a torch inside.

"Men, we're going to sneak up to the edge of the camp," Gideon told them. "Once we're there, watch me. I'm going to blow the trumpet, and when I do, you follow my lead and do the same." And so they did—breaking their pitchers and showing their torches and shouting, "The sword of the Lord and of Gideon!"

The Midianites and Amalekites freaked. They started fighting each other, then those who were left picked up and ran, with the Israelites hot on their heels.

As I said earlier, it sure seems to me like Gideon illustrates a lot of lessons we've already talked about in this book.

First, he *prayed*. Gideon's account is filled with his interactions with the Almighty: questioning Him (Judges 6:13, 15); asking for signs (verses 37–38); sacrificing to Him (verse 24); worshipping Him (7:15). Time after time, you read about God talking to Gideon, and Gideon talking to God. This is where everything in our relationship begins, and it's a crucial part of each and every step.

And here's another thing worth our attention: Gideon questioned God. He wanted to be sure that God was who He said He was and would do the things He said He'd do. Gideon might've had questions. He might've even had doubts. But they didn't disqualify Gideon from the work God had planned for Him. And God can use us too—even when we question. Even when we doubt. Listen, I know that Jesus told His doubting disciple Thomas that "blessed are those who have not seen and yet believed" (John 20:29 NKJV). But He didn't throw Thomas out on his ear. No, Thomas was really just beginning his journey following Christ: his doubts, like Gideon's doubts, were the start of his journey, not the end.

And in those prayers, Gideon saw what it meant to pray for the right things. He received *instruction* from God—smashing altars and Asherah poles, rallying the Israelites to battle. He learned that *managing* his meager resources was more important than a lightning-bolt *miracle*. Remember, God had been training him—from the time he was in that tiny winepress—to manage his resources well. Gideon found that *strategy* was more important than *stuff* when he divided his small force into three smaller units and, instead of giving them swords and shields, gave them trumpets and jars.

But for me, it's the people that stand out the most in Gideon's story. Instead of Gideon begging for *more* people, God encouraged him to make do with less. They just needed to be the *right* people.

Think about how Gideon separated his men, deciding who he was going to take into battle with him. It wasn't all that different from Gideon separating the wheat from the chaff. Gideon was doing that separation in a tight space—not physically maybe, but certainly mentally and emotionally. He was under as much pressure as he'd ever felt.

And then, while we're at it, think about the men he *did* select. Yes, cupping the water in their hands allowed them to be alert and aware of their surroundings. But metaphorically, it says something else to us today: They were literally holding precious resources too. While the other men greedily lapped up the water like dogs, letting the water run past them without a thought, the men who drank from their hands were physically holding what they needed. They were maximizing what they'd been given.

In praying to God, Gideon had accepted his mission. And he found that God had given him everything he needed to accomplish it.

God's blessings, like water, flow all around us. They can be our own resources of time and talent. They can be people too. So often we fail to see those blessings for what they are: miracles from God, to be managed carefully and expertly. So often we simply lap them up without thinking, without praying, without giving thanks for them. And sometimes we squander them, letting blessings slip right through our fingers and float away.

But when we live under God's direction and instruction, we think differently about things. We walk in His instruction bravely, without fear. We're aware not only of our surroundings but of the blessings that God has given us. And we cup those blessings in our spiritual hands like treasure—like the sacred gifts they are.

People are indeed sacred gifts. They are, very often, God's greatest blessings to us—and sometimes our greatest trials. Look at the relationships we read about in the Bible: Joseph's relationship with his brothers; Moses' "stiff-necked" people; David's family, friends, employer, and employees. Even Jesus' friends were afraid sometimes. Relationships can be painful, no matter what we do.

But Gideon shows us what to look for in good partnerships. He shows us a process for gathering the right people close to us—people who are unafraid, who are aware of their surroundings, who know how to manage what God has given them and hold those blessings in the cup of their hands. Ask people who they are—and listen to their answer.

You don't need an army at your back to do mighty work for God. You don't need a ton of people. You just need the right ones—people who love you, who love God and, like you, are trying to follow God's instruction for their lives. And with those elements in play, there's nothing you and your team—no matter how tiny it might be—can't do.

Now, let me ask you: Are you praying for the right people to fill that team? Are you praying to be the right person on *someone else's* team? Who have you had an influence on today? This week? This month? And is it the right influence? Are you living your life as God would want you to live—with your blessings cupped in your hand, watching for opportunities? Or are you just lapping up those blessings without a thought as to what God wants you to use them for? How have you been hurt by people? Have you prayed to God to heal that hurt? To forgive and move on?

CHAPTER SEVEN

How to Pray When You're Expecting a Miracle

I believe in miracles.

I am one.

I don't mean that in the sense that every life is a miracle (although it is). I mean it in the strictest, most supernatural sense. I shouldn't be here. Everything you've read shouldn't have been written. Everything I am and everything I've done shouldn't exist. No songs, no albums, no family, no Forward City. Travis Greene should not be.

And yet here I am.

I was born dead. I wasn't breathing. My skin was purple, my mother says. Doctors said I was stillborn. My mother and father didn't believe the doctor. They prayed. Oh, how they prayed. And a few moments later—maybe seconds, maybe a minute—I breathed. God performed a miracle.

Four years later my family was stationed in Germany (my father was an air force chaplain), and I fell out a window, four stories up. It didn't take long for the paramedics to come—but it was still too late.

I was pronounced dead. They put a white sheet over my body like a shroud, and that should've been the last of me.

But again, my mom wasn't having it. She picked up my lifeless body and prayed—prayed furiously over me that God would restore me to life. She called on Jesus once. And then again. And finally, she screamed for Jesus' help for a third time—asking that His blood might heal my body. And once again, when I had no business drawing another breath, I breathed.

I don't remember the fall or the revival. I was four years old. But my mom, she's never let me forget it. She's repeated that story again and again, and I've heard it countless times. And she says that, when I was leaving the hospital later, I told her a remarkable story: I told her I didn't hit the ground.

"A man caught me," I told her. "His face was so bright, so dazzling that I could barely look at him. 'Go home to your mama,' the man told me. 'This time you're going back to her. The next time, you'll come with me.'"

I asked the man his name.

"Jesus," He told me.

That was how four-year-old me made sense of what happened—the only way I could explain it to my mom. That was the only way I could describe the indescribable.

Don't tell me that miracles are all in the past—that God doesn't come down and do astounding things in our lives. My whole life is proof that He does. God is a God of miracles. He can do what He wants, when He wants, how He wants. And because God loves us more than a father loves his child, He does things for us that no scientist, no doctor, no professor can explain.

But sometimes we forget the other side of the coin. God is willing to do so much for us. But what do we do for Him? How do we manage the miracle?

I'm here because of God's miracle. But what good would that miracle be if I was on drugs right now? What good is that miracle if I jumped in front of a bus? What good is that miracle if I mismanage the miracle of life?

All of us have been given miracles, whether we see them or not. All of us have been blessed in ways we can't explain. Life *is* a miracle. Even as we think about praying for the right thing, our ability to pray at all is pretty amazing.

But we pray for other miracles too. A tumor to disappear. A relationship to heal. Life can be brutal sometimes. And while I believe that God can and does work in our lives in ways that science and the secular world would say are impossible, a lot of us know what it's like to pray for a miracle and have those prayers come up empty.

My mom prayed for me to live, and I did. But I know moms who've prayed for their own sons to live and . . . they didn't.

What do we do when we're praying for a miracle? What do we do when we're waiting for one? And what do we do if our prayers seem to go unanswered?

There's nothing wrong about praying for a miracle. Absolutely nothing. But as you pray for miraculous healing, pray for courage to deal with the sickness too. Don't just ask for a burden to be lifted, but ask for the strength to carry it—even if it never goes away.

That courage, that strength, that faithfulness in the middle of life's worst moments—those are miracles too. Even in the midst of all that pain, God can still work. Even in the middle of all that grief and suffering, God's love and grace and, yes, *blessings* can still shine through. You get up every day. You thank God every morning. You pray for the miracle. You pray with all your heart, knowing that

> WHAT DO WE DO WHEN WE'RE PRAYING FOR A MIRACLE? AND WHAT DO WE DO IF OUR PRAYERS SEEM TO GO UNANSWERED?

God can do anything. But you pray for strength and peace and hope in the meantime too. You pray for the power to push on and do whatever you can to clear the way for that miracle—and, in so doing, you let God work through you.

The quickest way to a miracle is to become one. The quickest way to a harvest is to sow. We see this all throughout Scripture. The widow became Elijah's miracle by feeding him when she and her son were in dire need of a miracle. She became for someone else what she needed for herself.

And the only way to a miracle? The only way to ask for the strength we'll need, whether or not it comes true for us? It's through prayer.

The Quickest Way to a Miracle . . .

In Acts we're told that "God worked unusual miracles by the hands of Paul" (19:11)—not just ordinary, everyday miracles but "unusual," or "special" (kjv) or "extraordinary" (esv). How extraordinary? People would bring him their handkerchiefs or aprons, and through those humble garments, Paul would actually heal their owners.

Acts 19 doesn't tell us what an "ordinary" miracle would look like, but it does suggest that miracles come in a lot of sizes. Sometimes they can be the sun-stopped-in-the-sky sort of miracle like we read about in Joshua 10:13. That is a supersized, no-doubt, uppercase MIRACLE. Sometimes miracles are smaller, like when we find just enough money to make the car payment. Some people might say that's not so much a miracle as a straightforward answer to prayer. And sometimes what *some* might call a miracle feels like just plain luck. When a math teacher tells his class that he's postponing the test till next week, that probably doesn't feel like an act of God to most of us. But for the student who forgot to study? That can feel miraculous! We use the word "miracle" a lot these days. Maybe we overuse it.

What's my definition of a miracle? It's when we see God in action—answering prayers that only He can answer, bringing healing to situations where healing seemed impossible. Those are miracles to me. Miracles are God's fingerprints on our lives. And you don't need to survive a four-story fall to see miracles in yours.

But when you take a step back and look at the world rationally and logically, you realize that, really, miracles are a dime a dozen. The fact we're here at all is way more improbable than the sun freezing in the sky.

Scientists say that the universe itself is curiously tuned to support life. Move a few variables (what physicists call "fundamental constants") by the teensiest of measures—the equivalent of a millimeter here or there—and our universe wouldn't exist at all. It shouldn't be here. The fact that it is, one writer for Medium said, equates to the probability of "tossing a coin and having it come up heads 10 quintillion times in a row."[1] And we haven't even started talking about a universe that could actually *support life*. The odds are so astronomically improbable that physicists who don't believe in God struggle to explain it. The latest theory in vogue—as any superhero movie fan will know—is the multiverse. In a creation made up of infinite universes, surely a few of them can support life, right?

And then think about the circumstances of your life. I told my mom that Jesus caught me. But chances are, if you're reading this book right now, Jesus caught *you* too. He might not have snatched you out of the air from four floors up, but He rescued you from a life of sin. And if He hasn't yet, He desperately wants to. He wants to give you that gift—the miracle above all miracles.

Yes, you *are* a miracle. It doesn't matter if you've been told otherwise—if someone in your life has said that you were worthless or a waste of space. The fact that you're here at all confirms what Psalm 139:14 says: "I will praise You, for I am fearfully and wonderfully made. Marvelous are Your works, and that my soul knows very well."

But how well do we really know it? Are we letting our own miracles go to waste? How are you managing that miracle?

Strong but Weak

Samson, whom we meet in Judges 13–16, was a walking miracle. He came at a time when Israel had, again, walked away from God. As a result, the nation had been under the thumb of the Philistines for forty years. Into this hopeless country an angel came, and he visited a man named Manoah. The angel told him that his wife would give birth to Israel's deliverer.

Just the fact that Manoah's wife would give birth *at all* was a miracle. She'd been barren for years. But to give birth to someone who could overthrow the hated Philistines? A people that had been in charge of the promised land for generations? That seemed impossible. And then when he grew—well, he was like a biblical superhero. We're told he killed a thousand Philistines with the jawbone of a donkey (Judges 15:15–16). If someone tried to tie him up, the ropes would heat up and break away (verse 14). He was like nothing that Israel or Philistia had ever seen, and the Philistines were desperate to stop him any way they could.

But this miraculous kid had some conditions to follow too. Samson was told that he should never drink wine or eat unclean food or—and this was really important—ever cut his hair. He was a Nazirite, a man consecrated to God.

But even though Samson was dedicated to serve God from birth, you get the feeling he didn't take that service all that seriously. He mismanaged the gifts that God had given him.

Early on in the story (Judges 14:5–18), we read about an example. Samson was on the road and was suddenly attacked by a lion, who clearly didn't know who he was messing with. Samson killed the lion with his bare hands—ripping it apart as "one would have torn apart a young goat." He continued on his way without giving the lion a second thought. But on his way back home after finishing up his business, he saw that honeybees had already made their own home in the lion's carcass. He reached in and pulled out some honey and ate it, and he even took some home for his parents. That's a big deal, because Samson, as a Nazirite, was not supposed to be touching dead things. And pretty soon, Samson was even *bragging* about it.

God's miracle was still in play. The Lord didn't take Samson's favor away—yet.

But when it comes to an unrepentant person, the Lord's patience has its limits.

By Judges 16:4, Samson had started hanging out with a woman named Delilah, who most scholars believe was probably a Philistine. As soon as the bigwigs in Philistia learned of her relationship with Samson, they bribed her to find out why he was so strong. At first, he lied to her. But eventually Samson told her the truth: "No razor has ever come upon my head, for I have been a Nazirite to God from my mother's womb. If I am shaven, then my strength will leave me, and I shall become weak, and be like any other man" (verse 17).

That's just what Delilah wanted to hear. She called in the Philistine leaders, lulled Samson to sleep, and had someone shave part of Samson's head. And when Delilah woke him up and told him that the Philistines were upon him, he found he had no strength to resist. He was captured, had his eyes put out, and was thrown into prison.

Mismanagement

Samson was guilty of the same thing we often are. We forget. Even after all He's done for us, we forget God. Even though our lives are miracles, we can forget His instruction. We forget *ourselves*. We lose sight of our plans, lose hold of our processes, lose our grip on our faithfulness. We reach for the honey when we know we shouldn't. We trust the wrong people instead of trusting God.

I've done it too.

I fell from a four-story window when I was four years old and fell into the arms of Jesus. When I was twelve, I prayed to God that, if He allowed me to do music, I would do it only for His glory.

But when I was twenty? I'd often forget that prayer. I had other things on my mind, other goals on my heart—and other distractions to follow. I still believed in God; that's never been an issue for me. I've never doubted His existence, never doubted that He saved me. But like a lot of people, I lost myself for a while. College is a time of tremendous temptation and distraction, and yeah, I got pretty involved in partying while I was at Georgia Southern University.

I didn't need a reminder that God is the God of the universe. But I needed to grow. I needed to come to a better understanding of God's love and grace. Once I got a real grip on God's character and His love for me, that sparked in me the desire to live for Him—and truly dedicate myself to Him.

We pray. God hears us. God answers us. God *gives*. What do we do with His gifts? How do we use them? Nothing is more tragic in this world than an answered prayer mismanaged. There's nothing sadder than not taking full advantage of what you've been given.

I believe that God sometimes withholds His miracles until He knows that we can manage them. You might pray for a bigger house, but what good is a bigger house if you don't keep it up? You might pray for a new job, but what good is that job if you don't know how to fill the role and use it to His glory? You might pray for more resources—but that takes us right back to the beginning of this book, right? What if you don't know how to wisely use the resources you've been given?

I believe that God wants to give you beautiful things, great things. His storerooms are full. He holds treasures in His hand. In Psalm 84:11 we read:

> For the LORD God is a sun and shield;
> The LORD will give grace and glory;
> No good thing will He withhold
> From those who walk uprightly.

Samson was a miracle. And honestly, he didn't completely waste his gifts. The Bible tells us that he was Israel's judge for twenty years, and he did a mighty work later. God supplied him with one last miracle—renewed strength—that was related to Samson's lifelong mission. Placed between two huge pillars in the Philistines' temple to their god Dagon, Samson prayed, and he found that he had the strength to bring that temple down (Judges 6:28–30).

Have you shown Him that you can be trusted with a miracle? Have you shown God that you'd know how to manage one if you got one? Have you made a plan? Have you walked in faith? God doesn't dance at your pleasure. He wants to bless you, but He wants you to own that blessing and to use it wisely.

How do you manage those miracles—be they the gifts you've been given from day one, the answered prayers you've received, or one of those extraordinarily rare, lightning-from-above *miracles* that confuse scientists?

Good Management Begins with Prayer

"But Travis," you say, "aren't you talking about *answered* prayers? Why pray *again*?"

But here's the thing: You need to pray for the right thing. And this time, the right thing is to say *thank you*.

When you're given a blessing, it's always important to say thank you, isn't it? Many of our mothers made us sit down and write thank-you cards after Christmases and birthdays. You can bet my own mom taught me to say thank you for every present, coin, or piece of candy I ever received.

When a massive miracle happens to us, of course we'll say thank you. We'll say thank you with tears streaming down our cheeks in that miraculous moment. But a year later? Five? We sometimes lose sight of the miracle, like I did in my twenties. We're grateful for answered prayers in the moment. But the next week, or the next year, we need another prayer answered. And we forget how God has been to us. If we're honest with ourselves, sometimes we're not that different from the Israelites—those "stiff-necked people" that Moses miraculously led out of Egypt. Even when God gave them manna—literally food from the heavens—they whined because it wasn't meat (Numbers 11:4–6).

Giving thanks for God's miracles and answered prayers is important—not only to show God how much we appreciate His gifts, but because it reminds *us* how much He's given us. We should start each day with a heart full of gratitude. We should say goodnight with our mind on how much we've been given.

Think about all the things that you should be grateful for: your family, the food in your fridge, the hot water running through your pipes. If you have a job you hate, be grateful you have it—even as you pray for another one. If you've got a friendship on the rocks, give thanks for that friendship and what it *was,* even as you pray for God to heal what it has become. Thank God for the miracles in your life. Thank Him for answering your prayers. Thank Him for your ability to draw breath and pray for more. *Thank you,* we should say. *Thank you.*

As you take that first step, take the second too. Remember that the miracles and answered prayers you've been given aren't all about you. They're about God. He answered your prayer. Now you can think about how you can use that answered prayer—that miracle—to answer other people's needs and prayers.

Or, if you want a more real-world example, turn to Acts 9. Saul, a Pharisee with a special zeal for persecuting Christians, didn't see three Christmas ghosts; he encountered Jesus Himself on the road to Damascus. It was a miraculous encounter, and it changed Saul's whole life. He changed his name to Paul and started traveling the known world to spread Jesus' message of the good news. Along the way, he performed miracles himself with the help of God— "unusual" miracles, as we saw in Acts 19:11. He also healed the lame (14:8–10), exorcised demons (16:16–18), and even raised someone from the dead (20:9–12). And we're not even talking about how many people have been saved by Paul's letters. His writings in the Bible have impacted me deeply. I bet they might've done the same for you.

That's what answered prayers should do to us. They're not just about giving us what we want. They're about changing our lives— moving us closer to the One who answered them. And if our lives are changed, we can be tools to change other people's lives too.

Look for opportunities to share your story of answered prayers like my mom did, encouraging other people with my own four-story story. If you've been handed a miracle, find ways to share it with others. Manage well what you've been given. Spread it around.

No and Not Yet

"But Travis," you say, "I have shown I *can* be trusted! I've made a plan! I walk in faith every day! Why am I not seeing the miracle that I need? Why are my prayers not being answered?"

Those are some of the hardest questions we can ask as Christians. And almost all of us, at one time or another, ask them. We've prayed for miraculous healing that hasn't come. We've prayed for new opportunities that never materialized. We've prayed for a son, or a daughter, or a dear friend to come to Jesus. And every day, those lost souls just seem to get more lost.

Why? we cry out. *Why?*

I don't know. But it's been a part of our faith since the beginning. The Psalms are filled with whys. Job is a book based on those whys. I fell from a window and was saved. That's a miracle. But prayer hasn't saved every child from getting hurt or dying. Christians die in car crashes and from cancer.

When God answers yes to your prayers, be prepared. Be grateful. Be ready to manage those answered prayers and, when you can, share them with others.

But sometimes God says no. Sometimes He says "not yet."

Sometimes it is, heartbreakingly, a flat no. We pray for a miraculous recovery from cancer and it doesn't come. We pray for a marriage to mend, and it ends in divorce instead.

Those are hard answers. When I was little, I know my mom prayed for my dad to stick around—to live. For her. For his kids. But God chose to take my dad home anyway.

I'll talk more about that part of my life later in this book, but here, I want you to know this: I understand how hard those *no* answers can be. They hurt. They can sometimes feel like your world's crashing down.

Maybe that's one of the lessons we can learn in the middle of the no. The world can feel like it's coming down around your ears, but it isn't. We move on. We wake up the next day. That day doesn't feel like a miracle for sure, in the middle of all that pain. But it still is. We're stronger than we think we are. And God's strength is with us too.

Paul knew suffering. He'd seen friends die for this new faith. He'd been beaten, thrown in prison, and eventually he would himself be killed. He knew all about God's miracles—and he knew that they didn't always come. But he believed and persevered anyway.

But sometimes what we *think* is a no is really a "not yet." God might be waiting for you, like He was waiting for me when I went to Charlotte. He wanted me to learn how to manage His miracle before He gave it to me. So if your prayers aren't being answered yet, think: Does God want me to learn something? Is He waiting for me? And truth is, sometimes God wants to teach you one of the hardest lessons of all: To wait. To be patient.

But we must be aware that God's timeline isn't ours either. How many generations of Hebrews in Egypt prayed for deliverance before they were delivered? How many years did Israelites exiled in Babylon pray to return to their promised land? How many *centuries* did enslaved African Americans pray for their freedom? How many folks *still* pray for real equality today?

God is always teaching through His "not yet." We can always learn while we're waiting—even though waiting can be so hard. Don't stand still when you're waiting, though. Learn. Lean into God. He hears your prayer. He loves you. Keep your faith. And keep praying. Keep praying.

And eventually that "not yet" just might become a yes. *Now you're ready,* God might say. And sometimes it can take the shape of a slow-motion miracle.

> WE CAN ALWAYS LEARN WHILE WE'RE WAITING—EVEN THOUGH WAITING CAN BE SO HARD.

Faithful Financing

You'll remember that in 2019 I prayed and prayed and prayed for a new building—a fresh start for Forward City. You'll remember that it didn't come to pass right away. God wanted to see how I managed before He answered my prayer.

In 2020, just as COVID was really digging its claws into the country, an opportunity came around. An old retail building—a 44,000-square-foot former Best Buy—came on the market. They were asking $1.75 million for it, which isn't a lot for a building that size. It helped that we're located in Columbia, South Carolina, where real estate prices are fairly reasonable. And the fact that the country was dealing with COVID helped too. Early in the pandemic not a lot of people were snapping up property when they couldn't even go outside without masks. I thought the former Best Buy might be perfect for Forward City—but I wouldn't have even considered it if it hadn't been for God. He told me that this was going to be our new building and Forward City's future home.

That March I announced to the church that we were going to buy that building. *How* would we buy it? That was a big question. The church had just $140,000 in the bank, and we were told that we needed to put down at least half a million dollars. That meant we needed to raise another $360,000 in just a few months. That's a lot of money for a church to raise—especially one that's still pretty young.

I knew we'd make it work—I had no doubt about that. Faith in God's goodness is something I've always had—even to the point that people around me sometimes tell me that I should be a little more realistic. But I knew that God had it under control. I had full faith in God's macro plan for us. But the micro plan? How it'd actually happen? I had no idea. I could see the big picture, but I couldn't see the blueprint. All I knew is that it would take a miracle.

All I could do was manage everything else the best I could. And that involved two important steps.

FIRST, I PRAYED. Every day I'd go over to the property and pray over it. It didn't matter if it was raining or the wind was blowing or it was ninety-five degrees. I'd leave my house, go to the Best Buy, and lay my hands on that vacant, roach-infested building.

SECOND, I WORKED. I reached out to every pastor under the sun that I knew. I called friends, athletes, celebrities—you name them, I called them. I think I dialed just about every number I had, asking for help. We put together a little fundraising campaign based on 2 Kings 4 (a story we'll be talking about later). We did everything we could to raise the money.

And the money came in. It didn't rush in all of a sudden. It wasn't like Forward City cashed a winning lottery ticket or that we got one huge donation from a willing donor. No, it came in bit by bit, trickle by trickle. Like the tide, the bottom line of our bank account was rising day by day, week by week. And after a few months, we had it—$500,000. We had our miracle.

We were thrilled. We were *celebrating*. God had done a mighty work, right? So we called the finance company in California to tell them we had the money.

"Yeah, about that," the finance company told us. "You know, because of COVID and prices and this and that and blah blah blah, the underwriters need just a tiny bit more."

"How much more?" we asked.

"You get us $750,000, and we'll finance the rest."

Well, the party stopped right there. Suddenly, without warning, we found we were still $250,000 short.

Was I worried? Not in the least. God had told us that this old, increasingly expensive building was going to be Forward City. I had no doubt. I told myself, *If I have faith for half a million dollars, I have faith for $750,000.*

So we got back to work, and I got back to praying. *I believe in You, God. I believe You can give us the $750,000 we need. I believe in this miracle.*

And yes, the miracle happened! Before long we had $750,000 in the bank. We had enough to put that down payment on the building and move Forward City forward! The celebrations began again, and we put another call into the finance company to tell them the good news.

"Yeah, about that," the finance company said. "There's so much going on, what with COVID and inflation and this and that and blah blah blah. . . . We need just a little bit more."

"How much more?" we asked.

"How about another $500,000?"

Another obstacle. Another wrench in our plans. It looked like our miracle was going to take more time, more work, more prayer, more everything.

I think that maybe people without a lot of faith might've thrown up their hands at this point. *It's not meant to be*, they might've said. *We'll wait.* They might've hunkered down in their own metaphorical winepresses while finances ran roughshod over their plans.

I knew this building was going to happen. I had faith in God's word—faith in God's miracle for us. I didn't have one sleepless night over raising the cash. I didn't wring my hands in worry. Sure, I did tell God that, if He didn't come through, I was going to look like a big idiot. But I was just joking; I *knew* God would come through. "God is not man, that he should lie," we read in Numbers 23:19 (ESV). "Has he said, and will he not do it? Or has he spoken, and will he not fulfill it?"

If anyone else was worried over raising another $500,000, I wasn't. In fact, I went the other way. "If we can raise $1.2 million," I said to my staff, "I believe we can raise the whole thing."

And we did.

In March 2020 I made a public commitment to buy that

44,000-square-foot building. By October, we had the $1.75 million to buy it. In *cash*. We paid the money and the place was ours, free and clear—no mortgage, no financing. Every wall, every window, every cockroach that scurried along those concrete halls was ours.

God still does miracles. You can literally bank on it. We did.

Made a Way

I believe in miracles. My son is one.

The year 2014 was looking to be an amazing one for Jackie and me. My music career, after years of struggle, was starting to get some momentum. My first live album—one that would eventually be called *The Hill*—was taking shape. And most important, Jackie was pregnant with our first child. We were going to be parents.

And then, in early April—just twenty-one weeks into her pregnancy—Jackie's water broke.

We rushed to the hospital, hoping against hope the baby was okay, that everything would be all right. But the doctors knew it wasn't. One pulled me aside and talked with me in the hallway. "Mr. Greene," she said, "I'm so sorry, but your baby's not going to make it." If he wasn't dead already, he surely would be in a matter of hours. And then she walked me through what was going to happen next—how they would take the baby from us and try to make the process as painless as possible. "I'm so very sorry," she said again. "The best thing you can do is go home and try again."

But Jackie and I weren't ready to give up. Not on our son. Not on God. We asked the doctor about other alternatives. And medically, we had just one: Jackie had to stay in bed. Just lie there and do nothing. No walks around the hospital halls, no trips to the bathroom. If we hoped to see our baby alive, that was the only way.

"But there's no chance," the doctor repeated. "Her water's broken, Mr. Greene. The baby is too small. He's going to die."

But we began to pray—pray for a miracle.

A high-risk specialist was quickly brought in, and she gave us a little hope. She said that she'd seen babies survive, even in such difficult conditions.

"It's been years, but I've seen this happen before," the specialist told us. "The baby has a chance—if she [Jackie] just lies here. We can give her steroids. We can try to contain things. Maybe the womb will stay in place. Maybe the baby can defy gravity. There's still some hope."

The odds were long. She suggested there might be just a 10 percent chance the baby would live—and even if he did, he might deal with intellectual and developmental disabilities that would plague him for the rest of his life.

But faith is a powerful thing. And we desperately wanted to see our son, alive and beautiful.

That kicked off the longest two months of our lives. Jackie spent the next seven weeks in bed—not just lying there but in what they called the Trendelenburg position. She lay flat on her back. Her feet were positioned to rest higher than her head to allow oxygen to flow to the baby and keep him alive. She was in that position so long that her legs were literally withering away. Doctors hooked her up to machines to keep her blood flowing and simulate at least some sort of activity.

I was in the hospital with her most of the time. I'd stay almost every night. Sometimes Jackie's mother would come to give me a little break—give me an opportunity to go home and take a quick shower. And then I'd be back at Jackie's bedside, praying. Praying that God would heal her womb. Praying for our little boy, struggling for life. Praying that God would see fit to give us one more miracle.

In that vigil—that long, hard time filled with the smell of disinfectant, the vending machines, the nurses who'd come and go in the day and dark—a song came to me. I started humming it a little. A little more. And then I picked up my guitar, and I began to sing. I called Jackie on FaceTime after taking a shower at her mom's house and began to sing to Jackie as she lay in that hospital room. As the machines around her beeped and whirred, I sang.

> Standing here
> Not knowing how we'll get through this test
> But holding onto faith, You know best
> Nothing can catch You by surprise
> You got this figured out and You're watching us now.[2]

That song became "Made a Way." It was just our little song at first—a song of hope and trust and faith that God would see us through. That God would work a miracle.

That song didn't stay in that hospital room, of course. I recorded it in November 2014. It found its own way onto my album *The Hill* and became, by the grace of God, one of the biggest gospel songs of the decade. It was number one on Billboard's US Hot Gospel Songs chart for thirteen weeks, and it brought me tons of awards.

All that was in the future, though. In that moment, as I played my guitar and sang, Jackie's and my focus was all on our son and on our God.

David Jace Greene was born on May 27—seven weeks after my wife's water broke. He spent another seven weeks in the neonatal intensive care unit. When we took him home August 1, we brought home oxygen tanks, too, so he could continue to breathe. One of my favorite pictures of him was taken shortly after he was born—beautiful brown eyes looking at the camera, oxygen tube fastened to his tiny nose, a blue knitted cap propped on his head.

Jace weighed two pounds eleven ounces when he was born. He could literally fit in the cup of my hand.

The miracle that God let drop from His own hand was so much bigger.

Don't Waste. Don't Wait.

At first doctors thought that Jace was deaf, but he wasn't. In fact, now there's no evidence that he was born premature. He's healthy. He's not perfect, because none of us are. He gets into trouble (sometimes he causes it). But he is, no doubt, a miracle. And every day of my life, I try to manage that miracle well.

We prayed for Jace, and God answered us. But what good is a miracle if I'm never there for him? If I'm always gone? If I never make his ball games? What good is a miracle if I'm just his *father* and not his *dad*?

Look around you. What are your miracles? *Who* are your miracles? Manage them well. Treasure them always. Never take a miracle for granted.

Sometimes we think miracles are just the inexplicable. The un-imaginable. But my definition of a miracle is a little broader than that. It can be as simple as making the right choice when everything in your body begged you to make the wrong one. It can be as soft as saying just the right thing to someone about to give up. You might not have seen her pain, but God did. And He sent you just in time.

We all know what that's like, I think: to read a Bible verse that you needed to read in that very moment. To hear a song that seems to echo exactly what your soul is singing. To hear a word of encourage-ment when you really need it. To get a hug when you feel like you're about to collapse. To get an unexpected check that covers your overdue electric bill *exactly*.

Most of us have seen such miracles. They might not make the

nightly news. They might not convince an atheist of a good and loving God. But we know miracles in our own lives when we see them. And you know what? God uses us as miracle workers too. Maybe we're the one who wrote the check, who gave that much-needed hug. When we follow God's instruction for our lives, we'll not just receive those unexpected blessings but we'll be able to give them, too, and that's what it means to become a miracle.

Let's think about what we've read in this book so far. How sometimes when we're praying for a miracle, we should be praying for something else instead. Instead of praying for money, pray for how to manage that money better. Instead of praying for stuff to miraculously fall from the sky, pray for a better strategy to deal with what you have. God believes in joint custody in His work. And while you might not look at what happened with Forward City after that SUV ride as a miracle, I sure do.

What's your definition of a miracle? Have you seen a real, huge, unexplainable miracle in your life? How did that change you? What prayers has God answered for you? What are you praying for that God is answering with "not yet"? What are you most grateful for?

Every day this week, I'd challenge you to do something. When you're getting out of bed, think of three things—big or little—and write them down and thank God for them.

CHAPTER EIGHT

Concentrate on What's Left—Not Who Left

My dad never stayed home from church. Never ever.

Willie Greene was an air force chaplain, and in 1989 he was serving at Robins Air Force Base in Warner Robins, Georgia. He and my mom were both ministers, and to miss church was just not done.

But one morning in early June that year he kept complaining about having an awful headache. "You go to church," he told us. "I'll stay home."

I remember him saying it like it was yesterday.

We went off to church, just as my dad said we should. But when we got home, his headache wasn't any better. It was so bad that my mom suggested the whole family take naps. My sisters were six and two years old, and my mom must have thought that if we all took naps the quiet would help my dad. She'd never said, "Hey, let's all take a nap." Not until this day. But we could see my dad was feeling terrible, so all us kids went to our rooms and into bed. Our nap was God's gift to our parents.

Then (as I later heard from Mom), Dad lay down on the couch, his head in Mom's lap.

"Read to me from the Bible," he said. And so she did. I can imagine her voice, reading softly and gently.

I woke up to the sound of my mom's panic. I came out of my room and saw Mom shaking Dad, trying to get him to wake up.

"Call 911, quick," she shouted to my older sister, Kim.

"No, don't!" I shouted. "They'll take him away!"

But the paramedics came, and I was right. They put him on a gurney and whisked him out. "Don't worry," my mom said. "I promise you, everything's going to be okay. He'll be back."

Years later Mom admitted to me that she knew everything wasn't okay. She felt Dad die in her lap. She felt him pass away as she read him Scripture. She knew that he wasn't coming back. And when Dad left, he took part of her with him.

But even if Dad was gone, his body lingered. The next time we saw him, hours later in the hospital, he was connected to a breathing machine. Tubes snaked around his hospital room. Mom called everyone she could think of to come say their goodbyes: his parents, my mom's siblings, friends—whoever could make it.

On June 6, 1989—two days after his aneurysm—Staff Sergeant Willie Ernest Greene Jr. was pronounced dead. He was just twenty-eight years old. He was buried June 11 in North Myrtle Beach, South Carolina. A week later, on June 18, we celebrated Father's Day without our father.

I was five years old.

The void my dad left behind is indescribable. His loss was massive to me. Massive. I grew up without a father. My dad never threw me a football or showed me how to fix a leak or taught me how to drive. I didn't have a father to help me navigate through puberty, to talk to me about girls and women. Sometimes I wonder what my life would've been like had Dad been around for my whole childhood. And I feel his loss—even to this day—in unexpected moments. I can probably count the times I've cried about my dad, but most of those have come when I wasn't expecting it. I'll feel the tears well up and I'll think, *Whoa, where did that come from? Why am I crying?*

Yes, the people who leave us leave a hole behind. They leave a mark. If I said otherwise, I'd be lying.

But God doesn't want us to fixate on who left. He wants us to remember what's left. And as I look over my life, there was a great deal left after my dad died.

Grieving Losses, Leaving Voids

So far in this book, we've talked a lot about plans and processes, answered prayers, and prayers we're waiting for answers on. We've talked about instruction and mission. How God can do amazing things for us and through us—but how He wants us to "help," giving what we have to the Lord's almighty works. We've talked about praying for the right things—process and strategy and management—and praying that when God's gifts come, we use those gifts to their fullest.

But sometimes it's not about management. It's not about process. It's about healing. It's about filling the emptiness left behind when someone left *us* behind.

We pray for a hole in our heart to be filled, a wound in our soul to be patched up. We pray for our broken homes and fractured relationships, for our wayward sons and daughters to return to us, for our friends to come to their senses. Most tragically, we pray to get over the grief and sorrow of those who've left this world permanently—those who've died and are never coming back.

In chapter 6 we talked about Gideon, who said goodbye to plenty of people as part of God's plan. Gideon needed the right people around him when he took on the Midianites. And just like him, *you* need to have people in your life who are unafraid and who are aware. You need people you can trust.

But that doesn't address the real, agonizing pain when people *do* leave, whether they walk out on their own or whether they're taken away from us. And that can be incredibly difficult to deal with. Because in the moment of that loss, we may feel that nothing and nobody can ever fill that gap.

Those deep, personal losses can twist us. We get angry and bitter. We can cry ourselves out of tears. We can curse our circumstances till we're hoarse. We can focus so much on what people did to us and how much it hurt that we stop really praying at all. Sometimes we get to the point where we're not praying for healing as much as we're praying for someone else to suffer. Our hurt turns to hate. Our broken hearts turn bitter. And every once in a while, we might even take it out on God Himself.

And here's the tricky thing. All that anger? All that bitterness? It can *feel good* to let it in, at least at first. Even soothing—like scratching a mosquito bite. *I've been treated badly. That guy's a jerk. How could he do that to me, after all I've done for him?* Hey, don't deny it. I know you've been there too. Instead of licking your wounds, you lash out at the person who hurt you—even if they're not around to feel it. You stew. You argue with them in your head. You think how much you'd like to see that person get what's coming to them. Caving in to all those negative feelings—nursing them, even—can feel like a trip to the masseuse. It feels good to want justice—to want vengeance, even. It's great when you tell your story of woe to other people and they say, "Yeah, you're right. They were wrong. They treated you badly." I've already talked about how hurt I can get when someone turns their back on me. Even when I understand why they left, it's hard. And when I don't understand, it's almost impossible. Only the grace of God can keep us from bitterness.

But as hard as it is to move on, we must. God tells us to. When you think about all the ways you've been mistreated or wronged, you lose sight of God's instruction. When you focus on who's *right*, you miss out on what's left. You can miss out on opportunities. You can even overlook the people in your life right now who *haven't* left, who *haven't* hurt you. When you focus on loss, you miss out on what remains.

When you scratch a mosquito bite, the focus of your whole world right then is on that itchy bump. But your mom was right: the only way to make a bite stop itching is to stop scratching.

> ONLY THE GRACE OF GOD CAN KEEP US FROM BITTERNESS.

Just a Little Oil

In 2 Kings 4 we meet a woman who's dealing with a tragic loss. Her husband died and left her with two sons and a mountain of debt. Back then, being in debt was even more serious than it is now. She couldn't declare bankruptcy. She couldn't go to her debtors and figure out a payment plan. Her husband sure didn't have any life insurance. Her options were very limited. The only thing she could do was sell her sons into slavery. It was a horrible thing to even contemplate. In those days, it's what some people resorted to.

Can you imagine that woman? Not only was she dealing with probably unimaginable grief, but she had to tackle an unimaginable crisis. Not only had she lost her husband, but she was on the verge of losing her sons as well.

But the woman still had one slim hope left: to see if the prophet Elisha might be able to help.

So she started telling him about how miserable her life had been lately. "My husband's dead," she told Elisha. "I'm all by myself now, and we don't have any money, and now my husband's creditors want to take my sons as slaves!"

I love what Elisha asked her next. It wasn't, "How much money do you owe?" or "How much money do you need?" He didn't reach into his back pocket for his wallet or ask for her Cash App information. Instead, Elisha asked, "What do you have in the house?" (2 Kings 4:2).

Maybe shocked that he would even ask, the widow told him, "We have nothing in the house except a small jar of olive oil."

Elisha said to gather all the jars and containers she could find. He told her to borrow as many as she could from her neighbors. Then the prophet instructed her and her sons to start pouring her oil into all the newfound jars.

And wow, did that oil pour. The widow and her sons filled up every jar, every container, every pitcher in the house. And only when everything that could possibly hold oil was filled to the brim did the oil stop. When all the vessels were full, Elisha told her to sell the oil to pay off her debts. And because there would be jars and jars of the stuff left over, she was to sell the rest and live on that.

What Elisha asked of the widow echoes what we've talked about in this book. First, it's important to manage what you have. Second, trust God to multiply that—to turn what you're managing into something so much bigger and greater than you'd expect.

Third, and most important, keep your eye on what you've got, not what you've lost.

We've got a lot of single moms in our church. Pretty much every church does. About a third of American children—twenty-four million, according to the Pew Research Center—are being raised by an unmarried parent, and it's usually the mom.[1] Broken families seem almost like the norm these days. Sometimes the fathers walk out.

Sometimes they're kicked out. Sometimes they're never in the picture at all. And no doubt, for the children involved, the loss or absence can be hard. Dads can be so important in raising a child. And let's be honest: Being a single mom is hard. Caring for kids when there are *two* parents in the household can be difficult enough. But to do it alone? That's a special kind of challenge.

But single moms have an amazing opportunity too. They have a chance to be, aside from God, the greatest influence on their sons' and daughters' lives. Moms can fill them with hope and encouragement and mirror God's love and grace. They can raise their children to be mighty men and women of God.

When Someone's Gone but Still Here

When we talk about who left, I want to extend the definition a little. Sometimes people leave without ever walking out the door. They're absentee parents even though they're right in the same room—checked out way too often on social media or too preoccupied with work to pay attention. They might be drunk most nights. Or high. Or just distracted.

A third of kids are being raised in single-parent homes, but another 15 percent of children are being raised in *neglectful* homes. In a study published in 2019 in the *Child Abuse & Neglect* international journal, those kids deal with higher rates of trauma and suicidal thoughts. They're also more likely to abuse alcohol and drugs.[2]

A lot of those kids make it through those difficult times and into adulthood determined to raise their kids better than they were raised. And many succeed. But the pain that neglect leaves behind is still real. It still hurts. Those damaged relationships lead to damaged people— and they can understandably lead to a lot of bitterness.

Many of those formerly neglected kids still have to deal with their parents now that they're adults. They might even be asked to take care of them—even though their parents rarely cared for them. How can children *not* be angry if a mom or dad lets them down? How can that not impact the relationship? Can you just let all that go?

Right here, right now, I'm going to write one of the hardest things you'll probably read in this book.

You've got to honor your father and mother. Maybe your parents hurt you. Maybe they weren't good parents. You still owe them honor. Jesus tells you to (Luke 18:20). If someone else said it, maybe you could skate around it. But when God says something, you should take notes. It doesn't come with any qualifiers or escape clauses. There's no asterisk on the Ten Commandments. You're supposed to honor your parents.

That doesn't mean you have to invite them into your house. That doesn't even mean you need to stay in a relationship with them. If your dad was using drugs when you were a kid, and he's still using drugs, you don't want him around your own kids.

But to *honor* someone is different from pretending that the relationship is problem free. Your parents may have been neglectful. They may have cut out on you. But you still owe them your honor. You owe them your respect. You owe them, even, your thanks. Because even if all they did was give you a share of their DNA, they were instrumental in making you who you are. And who you are is beautiful. Precious. Unique.

Honor isn't trust. But it is the ability to say, *I care about you. I love you.* And even, eventually, *I forgive you.*

When you're able to honor someone—someone who might've hurt you badly—it's a reminder of another important but *very* difficult truth: just as God has plans for you, God has plans for that person too.

God Sometimes Uses Those Who Use Us

We're all heroes of our own stories. We're the stars of our own lifelong movies. When something happens, it happens to us. And when people hurt us, they're the villains, right?

But here's the thing we forget: Our stories—as much as it might seem like they revolve around us—are actually part of a much, much bigger story. We're all characters in God's own book. And each one of us plays a part in that book. That includes you. And me. And the guy who cut you off in traffic. And the friend who stopped calling. And the son or daughter who cut off all contact with you. They might've done terrible things. They might even seem, right now, to be terrible people. But God still loves them— loves them in ways you can't even imagine. And He still has a place for them in His story—a part that He wants them to play.

In Jeremiah 29:11–14, God said,

> **OUR STORIES—AS MUCH AS IT MIGHT SEEM LIKE THEY REVOLVE AROUND US—ARE ACTUALLY PART OF A MUCH, MUCH BIGGER STORY.**

For I know the plans I have for you . . . plans to prosper you and not to harm you, plans to give you hope and a future. Then you will call on me and come and pray to me, and I will listen to you. You will seek me and find me when you seek me with all your heart. I will be found by you . . . and will bring you back from captivity. I will gather you from all the nations and places where I have banished you . . . and will bring you back to the place from which I carried you into exile. (NIV)

God told this to His chosen people, who were *literally* in exile at the time. But it's just as pertinent to us today. So often we separate ourselves from God, but He's still waiting for us. He still has plans for us. And as hard as it can be to hear (because I *know* it's hard to say), He still may have plans for the people you dislike, or people who dislike you. Remember, Jesus was surrounded by people who hated Him—and He *died* for them. Can't we find it in our hearts to be a little more forgiving ourselves? Especially since Christ directly told us to?

> But I say to you, love your enemies, bless those who curse you, do good to those who hate you, and pray for those who spitefully use you and persecute you, that you may be sons of your Father in heaven; for He makes His sun rise on the evil and on the good, and sends rain on the just and on the unjust.
>
> —Matthew 5:44–45

Are you okay with God using someone who used you? That's one of the most difficult questions a Christian can ask of himself or herself. When we're hurt, every instinct in our body tells us to hurt someone back. When some people smack their heads into an open cabinet door, they slam the door as hard as they can—as if the door will feel appropriately punished for hurting them. You stub your toe, and you're half tempted to kick whatever you stubbed it on—even though it's going to hurt you even more. The more it hurts, the more we want to hurt back. And the longer we nurse that hurt, the longer our anger and bitterness can fester and grow. Remember the old cliché that time heals all wounds? It's not always true. Anyone who has ever felt like they've been betrayed knows that some wounds continue to fester.

God commands us to forgive.

Jesus never got bitter. But even the Son of God was hurt as His hours on earth began to dwindle and the number of people leaving Him began to grow. In John 13:18–30 Jesus told the disciples that He knew all about the plot to betray Him to the Romans—and He knew who was behind it. Judas took a piece of bread that Jesus gave him and "went out immediately." John added a poignant visual for us too—so symbolic of this betrayal: "And it was night" (John 13:30).

That must've been the hardest hit for our Savior, but it wasn't the last. In Mark 14 Jesus told His disciples that they would all deny Him before the night was through (Mark 14:27). When Peter insisted he'd never deny Christ, Jesus said, "Assuredly, I say to you that today, even this night, before the rooster crows twice, you will deny Me three times" (verse 30).

Then, as if that wasn't enough, in the garden of Gethsemane Jesus begged Peter, James, and John to "stay here and watch" while He prayed (Mark 14:34). But three times when Jesus came back to see them, He found that every single one of them was sleeping. "Could you not watch one hour?" Jesus said in verse 37. I can imagine Christ's voice was full of sorrow and exasperation when He said it. Jesus knew that, before the rooster crowed, all of them would leave Him again. They'd leave Him before He'd leave them.

All Jesus' closest companions left Him that night, in one way or another. Judas left literally—breaking with the Son of God in an unmistakable way (even if the other disciples were a little confused about it at the time). They slept when Jesus really needed them. They ran away when the going got tough. That happens in our lives too. Like those neglectful or inattentive parents, sometimes our friends let us down. Our family can turn their backs on us. They walk away. They go to sleep. They deny us.

Jesus hurt, just as we all do when people go. And you know what Jesus did in the middle of it all? He prayed. In Matthew 26:36–46, Jesus prayed three times as His best friends fell asleep. In Luke 23 He prayed alone, on the cross: "Father, forgive them, for they do not know what they are doing" (verse 34 NIV). Who left Him? Everyone. But He prayed about what was left: the assignment. The sad, frightening, and glorious mission of the cross.

And here's the most amazing thing. Those disciples who fell asleep when Jesus begged them to stay awake? Those men who denied Christ when they promised they wouldn't? God wasn't done with them either.

Peter, who denied Jesus three times before the rooster crowed twice, became the leader of the early church—the "rock" that Jesus said he'd become (Matthew 16:18). James was killed by Herod, according to Acts 12—his passion for God apparently putting a bull's-eye on his back. John? He wrote a good chunk of the New Testament, from his own Gospel account of Jesus' life to three powerful letters to the book of Revelation. Christian tradition tells us that, outside Judas, all of Jesus' disciples made mighty contributions to the kingdom of God. They might've failed Jesus at a crucial moment. But God wasn't done with them. God used them.

And He can do the same for the people in our lives. The people who walk away. The people who leave us. The people who hurt us. God's not done with them either. "If My people who are called by My name will humble themselves, and pray and seek My face, and turn from their wicked ways, then I will hear from heaven, and will forgive their sin and heal their land," God said in 2 Chronicles 7:14. If people come before God with humility, God just might say to them, "Apology accepted. Now, let's see what you can do."

> IF PEOPLE COME BEFORE GOD WITH HUMILITY, GOD JUST MIGHT SAY TO THEM, "APOLOGY ACCEPTED. NOW, LET'S SEE WHAT YOU CAN DO."

It's a good lesson for us. For me especially.

I've talked about how much it hurts to have people walk out of my church. To leave my staff. I know what it's like to feel betrayed—to have people talking about you behind your back or saying things about you on social media. And let me confess something: Some of those same people are being used by God. Some of the same people who pulled as much as they could from me in terms of learning about ministry, learning about music—they're making use of everything they learned. They learned how to be musical at Forward City. They learned about how to operate a ministry. They took those tools, carried them out, and are using them in a different space. And they're using them effectively!

You can't wait for people to show gratitude, because a lot of times it never comes. And yet, however they left and for whatever reasons, God's still using them. People are coming to know Christ because of them. How can you be angry about that?

Well, honestly, it's *easy* to be angry. I'm human. But I'll tell you how I'm able to set it aside, and it has a name: the Holy Spirit.

It's the only way. You pray to the Holy Spirit. You lay all that hurt at His feet. You pray for what's left—because sometimes that's a part of what's left. The sadness. The anger. The sense of bitterness. You pray to set that aside so you can move on and do what God means for you to do.

But there's something else I've found that helps too: honesty.

"Honesty" has probably become my favorite word of the last three years. Listen, I am a Spirit-filled, Holy Ghost believer—a church boy through and through. I know how to be spiritual. But I don't know if I was ever taught to be honest. And one of the dangers we face in church is that we try to over-spiritualize the truth. We lie to ourselves about how we feel. We lie to each other. We smile and pretend that something doesn't hurt when it does. It can hurt like crazy. We can even lie to God—as if God was intimidated by the truth.

Psalm 51:6 says, "Behold, you desire truth in the innermost being" (NASB). So for me, over the past few years, I've been more honest with God, with myself, with my wife, and with my inner circle. When I'm meeting with the church's top leaders, I might talk about how hard it is to watch people go. "Man, this really hurt me," I'll say. "I didn't want this person to leave our staff." Or "I'm so disappointed we weren't able to hire so-and-so. I'm so sad he declined our offer."

Sometimes it goes even deeper: "Guys, God's been dealing with me in the realm of jealousy," I might say during a morning staff devotional. "I've really been struggling with it lately. I'm jealous of this guy and his success."

Staff members will look at each other.

"So it's okay to be jealous?" someone might ask.

"No, it's not," I'll say. "But that's what I'm dealing with. That's what I'm praying for God to help me with right now."

It's pretty intimidating at first to be that transparent. But man, when I started putting that stuff out there—sharing some of those hard, honest truths—it made a huge difference, both in me and in our church.

For me, the more I started confessing these difficult emotions, the better I felt. Lighter. It was like letting the steam off a pressure cooker or squeezing out a little water from an overfilled water balloon. The more I started letting out, the more it started getting out. Sometimes we hold on to all these negative emotions. We hoard them, like they're treasures. Jesus never did that. He told His disciples about His sadness, His disappointment, that night in Gethsemane. We must open the door. We need to allow all that anger and bitterness to walk out—and for the healing grace of Jesus to step in. Talk about your struggles in safe environments and let everything out. The more I let out, the less space it took up inside me. The more I let out, the more space I had for better, more productive emotions. The more space I had for God to work.

But it made a huge difference in our church too. Our staff members know that I'm human. They don't see me as a robot. And it gives them a safe environment to be honest with me—to share their own hurts and struggles and trials.

Funny how the right sort of prayer, and the right sort of attitude, can change the whole narrative, isn't it? All that hurt over people leaving the church—through the Holy Spirit and some old-fashioned honesty, it brought a lot of us closer together.

That can be the same with you too. When someone leaves you, don't ignore the hurt. Don't pretend it's not there. Pray about it. Lay it at God's feet. Be honest with Him—and be honest with your friends and family about it too. Let it out.

What's Left

I missed my dad growing up. I still miss him. But my childhood isn't filled with a ton of trauma. And I can only give the credit to two people: God and Mom.

Willie and Charleather Greene met in high school and got engaged right here in Columbia, South Carolina—ten minutes up the street from Forward City. My dad was my mom's first and only boyfriend. When the Lord called my dad home, she was devastated. Growing up, I remember hearing her cry. She'd pray with us before putting us in bed, tucking us in, and kissing us good night. And then, when we kids were quiet and the house was still, she'd weep downstairs. I can still hear her crying.

Sometimes I would creep down the stairs and see her. "Are you okay, Mama?" I'd ask. She'd smile through her tears and tell me to go back up to bed and reassure me that everything was fine. She was sad, that's all.

But the pain of a loss like that never truly leaves us. Mom didn't cry as much as time went on. But on their anniversary? His birthday? Decades later it would still hit her hard. Even today, more than thirty-four years after my father died, my mom can barely talk about him without weeping.

But she's the living example of weeping at night and waking up joyful in the morning (Psalm 30:5). As much as she wept over who left—my dad—her attention focused on who was left: me and my sisters. She built her life around what was left. We became her everything, and she made sure our lives were filled with laughter. Christmases must've been incredibly hard on her, but for us kids? Mom made Christmas a party. Family vacations were a blast. Yes, I missed my dad growing up. For so many reasons and circumstances, I wished he could've been around to teach me, to play with me, to be with me, but when I look back on my childhood, I don't look at the loss. I look at the love. I look not at what I lost but at how much I had—thanks to my mom.

When I said earlier that single mothers have a tremendous opportunity raising their children, I'm living proof of that. I grew up with a lot of women. Good Lord, a *lot* of women. But women, I think, are smarter than men, and that forced me to be smarter too. I think it made me a quicker communicator. I likely have better discernment than I otherwise would've, being raised in the environment that I was and with such great teachers. Maybe I'm even a little bit more orderly.

Mom raised me in a house with a lot of rules. I didn't spend the night at many other kids' houses, so they spent the night at mine. Many of the movies that everyone else watched I never got to see as a kid. And when I see them now, as an adult, I realize I didn't miss much. Mom made sure I was respectful, that I ate right, that I worked hard in school. And while I might have thought, as a kid, that our house had too many rules, they helped sculpt me. They molded me. They *filled* me.

My mom is the widow in 2 Kings, man. She focused on the oil. She used everything that she had. And through her love, she multiplied it. The oil continued to flow in the form of her children.

My wife's mom, Cynthia, is an amazing woman too. Jackie's all about the oil. Our mothers weren't carrying babies. They were carrying *nations*. Jackie's the co-pastor of Forward City, a phenomenal speaker, incredible teacher, and the love of my life. Her ministry has reached countless people. Her book *Permission to Live Free: Living the Life God Created You For* will change the lives, I think, of everyone who reads it—and all my wife's gifts and outreach can be traced to her mom.

My mom didn't just birth me. She birthed my music ministry. She birthed this church. She birthed this book. After Dad died, she focused on what was left.

And the jars were filled.

For more than twenty years, my mom has preached in prisons. She visits several prisons in the area monthly—feeding, teaching, leading ministry, helping others lead. I've been going with her ever since I was eighteen years old—about two years after she started going herself. When I first started helping her with her prison ministry, it was a little intimidating. With three to four hundred convicts packed into a gym, it feels a little scary to someone who's not used to it. But now when I go, it's almost like going home. All the inmates know me. Some have known me for twenty years. They know my story; I know a lot of theirs.

And Mom loves it. Absolutely loves it. It's one of the highlights of her life. It's another way that the oil multiplies around her. And she teaches the prisoners to multiply the oil too.

You don't think oil pertains to prisoners? You don't think the story works for them? Think about those people in prison for a minute. Their lives are, in a lot of ways, defined by *who left*. How did they wind up in prison? Maybe their dads left them. Maybe their moms did—if not physically, then emotionally. Maybe they've experienced their own betrayals, their own feelings of abandonment. Some female prisoners were locked up when they were pregnant and had their babies taken away. Can you imagine that? Can you imagine a child being taken away from her mother?

If they were raised in a great home, then perhaps *they* were the ones who left. They left their lives, their friends, their futures. After making one bad decision, or several of them, they were ripped away from a life that could've been. And some are never going to see the world from outside those prison walls again. They'll live there and die there.

Truthfully, those inmates failed people to get where they are. I'm sure most have friends and family who still grieve for them. Some are angry. Some are bitter.

But you know what? My mom believes that God's still working in them—working even inside those prison walls. "He has sent Me to heal the brokenhearted, to proclaim liberty to the captives, and the opening of the prison to those who are bound" (Isaiah 61:1). Walls cannot keep them from the love of God. Iron bars cannot keep them from the freedom found in Christ. He has plans for them even now. My mom doesn't believe those words go cold just because you're in prison.

Those inmates can dwell on who left them, or who they left. But my mom, she encourages them to think about what's left. Because even in those cold, gray prisons—even inside those iron bars and walls topped with razor wire—oil is there. Oil in the form of peace. Of forgiveness. Of teaching their own children to steer clear of those walls and find a better way. Oil can still flow. Good can still be done. God can still be seen, working in the lives of the people that so few others see.

It's not just prisoners who need forgiveness. It's those who left us. Those who forgot us. And we need forgiveness, too, for the people we might've hurt or forgotten along our way.

Who left you? Who hurt you? Or let me ask, who have *you* left? Have you begged forgiveness of someone who might need to forgive you?

Don't look back at all those hurts, all those regrets. Look forward. Pray differently. Look toward healing. Look toward the oil in your life, and remember: whatever is left, God can multiply.

CHAPTER NINE

When God Calls an Audible

You probably haven't heard of Charles Thomas Studd. But back in the day, he was cricket's version of LeBron James.

Cricket?! you're asking. *Why are we talking about cricket?* But stay with me here. Cricket's not exactly a top attraction in the US. But in the United Kingdom and a lot of other places, the sport's a *huge* deal. Back in the late 1880s, cricket (which uses a bat and ball, and many say was the forerunner of baseball) was an absolute obsession. And Studd—referred to in the papers as "C.T."—was a national celebrity.

The youngest son of a wealthy jute and indigo planter, C.T. was already drawing national notice as a cricket player when he was just sixteen years old. By nineteen he was captain of the cricket team at Eton College. By 1882, when he was just twenty-two, he was the leading batsman in the British Isles and participated in what was arguably the most famous cricket match in history—albeit on the losing side. C.T.'s England team lost to Australia, which inspired *The Sporting Times* to write a mock obituary for English cricket: "The body will be cremated, and the ashes taken to Australia," the obit read. Since then, the England–Australia series has been called The Ashes, with the winner receiving an urn.[1] The word "ashes" might've described C.T.'s spiritual life around that time.

The guy seemed like he had everything a young Victorian-era gentleman could want. He was a great athlete. He was famous. And thanks to an impending inheritance, he was soon to be rich; he was expected to inherit 25,000 British pounds[2]—the equivalent of about five million dollars today[3]—when he turned twenty-five in 1885. But even though he'd become a Christian in 1878, his faith hadn't really come alive. Later in his life C.T. wrote, "Instead of going and telling others of the love of Christ, I was selfish and kept the knowledge to myself. The result was that gradually my love began to grow cold, and the love of the world began to come in. I spent six years in that unhappy backslidden state."[4]

But that changed in 1884 when C.T.'s brother, George, grew seriously ill, which triggered some deep introspection in C.T.'s own life. As he grappled with his brother's sickness, C.T. went to hear D.L. Moody, a famous evangelist, preach. C.T. was probably like a lot of lost souls who wander into Forward City any given Sunday morning—filled with questions and doubts and searching for a little hope. It's in those spaces, when people feel empty, that God does His best work, and so it was with this young cricket player. That night, C.T. changed. He came to see Christ in a new way, and that became the catalyst for a stunning reversal. He decided to drop the cricket bat and pick up the Bible: C.T. would go to China as a missionary.

The cricket world was shocked. His family was flabbergasted, and his own mother was dead set against it. The decision might've surprised even C.T. He knew all that he was giving up to do what seemed crazy to most people. "But I knew God had given me His marching orders," C.T. later wrote. He wound up giving away almost his entire fortune and spent most of the next forty-five years working as a missionary in China, India, and Africa, introducing countless people to Jesus and the gospel. He died in 1931 in Ibambi, a city in the Democratic Republic of the Congo.[5]

As a former cricketer, C.T. was probably used to changing his sports strategy on the fly. And maybe that's why he could hear God's audible so clearly, instructing him to change course.

Getting a New Play

You know what an audible is, right? We get the word from football. Every play on offense is, essentially, a little mini plan. The coach, or sometimes the quarterback, tells the players exactly what they're supposed to do. One receiver, for instance, might be asked to run ten yards down the field, stop, and wait for the ball. That tight end will run a hook route. The center will block that guy. The guard will pull this way. The quarterback will take five steps back and throw. In professional football, that one play is the result of hours of work and practice and film study—a play the coaches feel will work well in a particular game and situation.

But here's the thing: There's another team on the field, too, and they have their *own* plan in place. The quarterback might go to the line of scrimmage, look at how the defense has positioned itself, and say, "Uh-oh, our play isn't going to work." So right there, on the fly, he calls an audible—barking out a *different* play that he hopes will work better given the circumstances.

We have all received audibles in our lives, and sometimes we call our own. We need to change direction at work or home. We need to pivot from one project to another. But very often God calls audibles for us—pushing us in ways that we didn't expect. Those audibles might change our days or our lives. God might call us, like C.T., to give up everything to do something for Him that seems crazy. Or He might call us to *make* tons of money so that we can use it for His purposes. He might ask us to give up fame, or He might ask us to embrace it to further His design. He might ask us to change careers. Move to another country. To invite someone down on their luck into our home for Thanksgiving. To preach the gospel to a stranger in the supermarket line. To let go of someone. To *forgive* someone.

Honestly, listening for God's audible can be pretty scary. In John 15:11 Jesus said, "These things I have spoken to you, that My joy may remain in you, and that your joy may be full." God wants to give you *joy*. But it doesn't say He wants you to be *comfortable*. Look at the stories we've already gone through, and you can see that the audibles He calls make His followers pretty uncomfortable indeed.

We've talked a lot in this book about how God likes you to take part in His works. It's good to pray for what we want and need, but we need to remember it's for His glory, not ours. We need to let God know that we're serious, and that we're preparing ourselves to use His gifts. Write our plans down (Habakkuk 2:2–3). And if our desires are aligned with God's desires, wow. Special things can happen.

AND IF OUR DESIRES ARE ALIGNED WITH GOD'S DESIRES, WOW. SPECIAL THINGS CAN HAPPEN.

But what if you ask God for an apple and He gives you an orange? What if you ask for a new job and He gives you one . . . in Dubai? Are you prepared to hear an audible from God? Are you prepared to follow what He tells you to do?

A New Play Comes In . . .

Read the Bible, and it's hard to find characters who *didn't* hear an audible. You meet all sorts of people who were just minding their own business when God tapped them on the shoulder and pointed to a new path.

Noah, build an ark.

Gideon, lead an army.

Mary, bear a Son.

It wasn't necessarily easy. At best, folks may have pointed at them and laughed or told them they were a little crazy. At worst, they risked their lives to follow God's audible. But few folks in Scripture risked more—or, ultimately, gained more—than Jesus' twelve disciples.

Four of them (Simon Peter, Andrew, James, and John) were fishermen (Matthew 4:18–22). They probably didn't have easy lives, but they knew what they were doing. And then God told them to "follow Me, and I will make you fishers of men" (verse 19), and they did just that. Matthew, a tax collector (10:3), probably did lead a luxurious life. But he gave up his nice dinners and comfy bed for long hikes, rough nights, and maybe days where he was hungry. I don't think that life following Jesus was easy. But once Matthew started, he never seems to have hesitated.

But I'm not sure if anyone in the New Testament followed as many audibles as Simon, who'd come to be known as Peter.

That first audible was amazing. Jesus said, "Follow Me." And Peter and Andrew did just that: "They immediately left their nets and followed Him" (Matthew 4:20).

Throughout the Gospels, Peter seems to have been an excellent audible follower—even if he sometimes had his own ideas of what play the Almighty should call. (Don't we all?)

In Matthew 14:22–32 we read that the disciples were in a boat in the middle of the stormy Sea of Galilee. They'd left Jesus on shore to be alone for a while and pray. But during the "fourth watch" (sometime between 3 and 6 a.m.), the disciples saw Jesus walking across those waves toward the boat. Weird, right? The disciples thought so, too, and assumed they were seeing a ghost until Jesus told them it was Him.

So Peter—maybe wanting to be doubly sure that it was indeed Jesus—said, "Hey, Lord, if that is You out there, tell me to come out there with You on the water!"

So Jesus said simply, "Come" (Matthew 14:28–29).

It was a clear audible, and Peter stood up. He put one foot outside the boat and *onto* the churning waves. He took his other foot and planted it *right on top of the water*. And just like that—keeping his eyes focused on Jesus—Peter started to walk.

For a while, everything went (pardon the pun) swimmingly. And then Peter made the mistake of thinking about something other than Jesus. He started thinking about the vicious wind and started to sink. "Lord, save me!" he shouted. And with those words, Jesus reached out His hand and caught Peter from going under, saying, "O you of little faith, why did you doubt?" (Matthew 14:31).

It's a great illustration of what can go wrong with audibles. And when it comes to God's audibles, the problems are never in the play call. They're in us. Instead of focusing on what the Lord is calling us to do, we focus on all the things that could go wrong. We get caught up worrying about life's winds and waves. We start thinking, *Hey, I'm not supposed to be able to do what God's asking me to do! It's impossible!*

And then we start sinking. We get in over our heads.

Focus on Jesus. Always.

I knew God had plans for me. Big plans.

When I was seven years old, my mother told me that my music was going to take me around the world. She wasn't the only one who said it. I heard it from a whole lot of preachers. When I played music around the house, people who came over would tell me, "Man, that is so amazing. You're so talented. You've *got* to do this for a living." So honestly, I just bought into the hype.

Believing—in God, in myself, in answered prayer—has never been an issue for me. Wrapping my mind around God's *what*—as in *what* He's got in store for me—has never been a stumbling block. I live in a place of confidence. When I dig into finances at work or at home with my wife, I'm always the guy who says, "Everything's going to work out. God's got it." And Jackie says, "Yeah, God's got it. But also, we need to make a budget."

That budget? The plans? The strategy? That's the *how*, and it's a big part of what this book's about. Trusting in the *what*, but working in the *how*.

But that *how* part can be awfully hard. My stories from North Carolina hopefully illustrate how hard it was for me. Yeah, I still believed God had big plans for me. He had a mission that involved my music. And I never doubted it. Not even for a sec—

Well, that's not exactly true. I didn't doubt God. I didn't doubt His instruction for me. But I'm only human. And the only times it got difficult for me—the only times when doubt started trying to worm its way in—were when I looked at other people.

It reminds me so much of Peter, walking on the water. As long as my eyes were on Jesus, I stayed afloat. But the moment I looked around and saw some other successful people around me, I'd start comparing myself to those people. I started judging my own career based on their successes. It was in those moments that I started sinking into depression, into sadness. "When is it my turn?" I asked God.

I didn't doubt the *what*. But I was frustrated by the *when*. And that's when I could feel myself sinking.

Those days weren't often. But there were enough of them to remember. And I'm glad that I do. Looking back, I'm glad I could see what a difference my focus made. When I keep my eyes on God, I know that nothing is impossible. When I look at my life's wind and waves, when I start listening to doubt and depression, that's when I sink.

I think that happens to us all, doesn't it? Life is challenging. And when we hear an audible, it's hard to step out of the boat. We see the water rise and swirl. We hear the wind howl around our ears. We hear God's call, but we are scared to follow Him. We lose sight of Him. We get afraid.

Do you feel like you're hearing an audible from God now? Is He calling you into a new mission? Is He giving you a new instruction? Is He telling you to follow a crazy dream, like He told me to pursue my music? Or is He asking you to give up some worldly success for a better call, like He did C.T. Studd? Or is He simply giving you the same audible He gave the disciples: *Follow Me. Follow Me more closely. Follow Me more dearly. Follow Me like your life depends on it—because it does. Follow Me.*

When Jesus called Peter to walk on water, that wasn't the last time that he heard an audible. Jesus had plenty of surprises in store for him and the rest of the disciples. Perhaps the biggest was something called the Great Commission, when Christ told them to "make disciples of all the nations, baptizing them in the name of the Father and of the Son and of the Holy Spirit, teaching them to observe all things that I have commanded you; and lo, I am with you always, even to the end of the age" (Matthew 28:19–20). That was a huge audible. Peter was never going back to fishing. He was going to be, in Jesus' words, "the rock [on which] I will build My church, and the gates of Hades shall not prevail against it" (16:18). Peter would go on to heal the lame (Acts 3:1–11), raise the dead (9:36–41), and be whisked out of a prison by an angel (12:7–17). And according to Christian tradition, Peter ultimately died for the audible entrusted to him by Jesus—a sacrifice he was grateful to give.

It's funny when you look at Peter's story, because sometimes the guy messed up those audibles. When Jesus called him out onto the water, Peter didn't walk for long. He sank. But he learned from that experience. He learned from his other failures too. And ultimately, Peter became, just as Jesus had predicted, the cornerstone of the Christian church—one that currently includes more than two billion people and continues to grow.[6]

But for my money, I'm not sure if there's anyone in the Bible who learned more from his audibles than Moses. And even though we've touched on his story, I want to show you what I mean. Because when we're talking about audibles, Moses' life is full of them.

A Good—and Boring—Start

Moses began his life—or at least the life *he'd* remember—in the most luxurious surroundings you could imagine. Admittedly, he was originally born to humble Hebrew parents in ancient Egypt, who put him in a waterproof basket and set him in the Nile for his own safety (Exodus 2:3). But when Pharaoh's daughter saw the basket, got a look at the kid, and decided to raise him as her own, Moses wanted for nothing.

For the next forty years, after he was drawn from the Nile, Moses was in Pharaoh's palace—living, literally, like a prince. He was eating the best food, drinking the best wine, learning all about Egypt, and maybe learning how to rule. He was clearly a powerful man. Moses might have been a little like C.T. Studd, when you think about it—only more so. He had everything he could want. Money. Glory. Comfort.

Then he made a mistake. And Moses' whole world was taken away in the snap of a finger.

The story picks up in Exodus 2:11, where we're told that Moses "went out to his brethren and looked at their burdens." That's important, because right there we know that Moses knew he was a Hebrew—just like the slaves working for his adopted grandfather. He knew that, while he was living in luxury, his people were suffering. And then Moses saw a fight—an Egyptian beating "a Hebrew, one of his brethren," reiterating Moses' pull to defend a fellow Hebrew. "So he looked this way and that way, and when he saw no one, he killed the Egyptian and hid him in the sand" (verse 12).

I don't think that this was *God's* audible. This was Moses—and he stepped offsides here. He wanted to protect his people, which is great. He had a deep passion for justice, which is outstanding. But passion without wisdom is deadly in every respect. And wisdom begins, *always*, with God.

Killing the Egyptian wasn't something that God had asked Moses to do. God didn't make Moses do it. Throughout the book of Exodus, we read plenty about what God says and what God does. But here, God hadn't said anything. This was *Moses* at work. And while he was, on one hand, doing something worthy and noble—trying to help someone who was being abused at the hands of someone else—God never asked him to do it.

Man, that sounds just like us, doesn't it? Sometimes we let our passions get away from us. We let our desires master us. Sometimes what we try to do on our own initiative and in our own strength is good. An outsider might even look at it and call it moral. But if God's not in the picture, it can backfire in a big way. As Proverbs 14:12 says, "There is a way that seems right to a man, but its end is the way of death."

Are you trying to fix something in your life without God's help? Without God's audible guiding you? That can lead to problems. Moses, like Peter, took his eyes off God. He looked at his surroundings and responded to *them*—not to his Lord. And so the life he knew just . . . sank.

But at the risk of spoiling the story, here's an encouraging thought for those of us who might find ourselves sinking because we made a similar mistake before God—which so often leads to bigger, more obvious mistakes. Just as Jesus was there to catch Peter when he took his eyes off Christ, God was there for Moses too.

Yeah, we make mistakes. And when we pay for those mistakes, it can look like our lives are coming down around our ears. But God's still with us. And He can still speak into our lives if we listen. He can still call an audible.

> **GOD'S STILL WITH US. AND HE CAN STILL SPEAK INTO OUR LIVES IF WE LISTEN.**

In the Wilderness

That Egyptian that Moses killed didn't stay hidden for long. In Exodus 2:14 Moses learned that someone saw his violent act. By the very next verse, Pharaoh himself knew. To save his own life, Moses ran away from his life of luxury.

It's interesting how quickly, in the Bible's verbiage, Moses' entire life changed. In Exodus 2:14 he was still a prince of Egypt. By verse 15 he was on the run—fleeing from Pharaoh who, yep, wanted to kill him. Two verses later Moses was making friends with the daughters of a guy named Jethro. Soon after, he was embarking on a new career as a shepherd.

Audibles can be shockingly swift and sudden. But we don't hear them all the time, and it can take a long while before we hear another one. They come like lightning strikes on your front lawn—they're unmistakable when they come, but they just don't come often.

For Moses, it took forty years. All that time he was a fugitive—hiding out in the land of Midian. He was a veritable prisoner—not physically but *mentally*. He wasn't a prince anymore. He was a shepherd, taking care of someone else's sheep. He was a prisoner of his own actions. Just as we are sometimes.

I think about the prisoners my mom ministers to—how their own actions put them where they are. I think about people who made bad financial decisions when they were younger that locked them in a prison of debt. We can be free as a bird and jailed by our own addictions or sins. We can be chained by so many things, even when we never see a single chain or manacle.

That reminds me of Peter again—and another time he listened to a message from heaven. He was in prison in Acts 12:6–7, bound, we're told, by two chains: "Now behold, an angel of the Lord stood by him, and a light shone in the prison; and he struck Peter on the side and raised him up, saying, 'Arise quickly!' And his chains fell off his hands."

Who unlocks those chains, whether they're literal ones, like Peter's, or more metaphorical, like so many of ours? God does. And God freed Moses from his own metaphorical prison too—with one of history's most powerful audibles.

The audible came on what felt like an average day. In Exodus 3 Moses was tending his father-in-law's sheep, just like he had every day for the past four decades. But as he and those sheep were on Mount Horeb, Moses saw a burning bush. Now, that's probably not unheard of in Midian: bushes do catch on fire. But we're told that despite the fire, the bush was just fine.

The experience would get more shocking yet: the bush—or rather *God*—addressed Moses by name in Exodus 3:4.

Moses, Moses!

And what did Moses say? "Here I am." He heard the audible.

He was eighty years old by that time—but just a shepherd. Yet Moses' own experience was exactly what God needed. The world might've seen a shepherd, but God called an audible because He knew Moses was a leader.

If Moses felt that his time in Egypt was wasted, God knew better. In that time, God had taught him about infrastructure and government. He learned how to manage resources and people. He learned what it took to lead a *nation*. (He even learned how to read and write, which would later be useful in writing portions of the Torah—the first five books of the Bible.) Not one second of Moses' forty years in Egypt was misspent. God used it all.

Now think about those forty years that Moses spent in Midian. He learned how to survive in the wilderness. He knew what plants to eat and how to find water; how to start a fire, sleep on the ground, mend his own clothes, and fend off wild animals. He learned how to live outside the palace walls, how to do without. And he learned how to care for a flock of living things that didn't know which way to go. Through those sheep, Moses taught himself how to prod, how to guide, and—most important—how to bring that flock safely home. That experience as a shepherd surely would come in handy over the next forty years as he guided a flock of stiff-necked Hebrews through unfamiliar country and unimaginable hardships to the promised land.

Moses was a prince and a wanderer. He was a ruler and a shepherd. He knew the palace and he knew the wilderness. When Moses turned eighty, he must've thought that his entire life had been wasted and squandered. But God had given him exactly the tools he needed to fulfill His instruction, and he became one of the most important people in history. It's as if Moses collected a grain of sand for each day of his life and put it in a bag—and at the end of eighty years, he opened it and found the bag glittering with diamonds.

But it took God's audible for him to open that bag—to truly put the instruction into motion. From the burning bush the Lord spoke: "I am the God of your father, the God of Abraham, the God of Isaac, the God of Jacob. And I have a job for you."

We've talked about how, after all that time in Midian, Moses tried to reject God's instruction. "Who am I that I should go to Pharaoh, and that I should bring the children of Israel out of Egypt?"

But God saw Moses' strengths, that he had all the essential tools for the glorious work ahead.

We pray. We pray for our mission. We pray for our God to give us instruction. We pray that God might use us in His perfect work. We pray for the *right things*.

But we know—know so painfully—how imperfect we are. Maybe we feel unequal to what God is calling us to do. Maybe we're not scared of receiving an audible; maybe we feel unworthy of hearing it. And our doubts are reinforced in a thousand ways. We shout at our kids when we shouldn't. We make a mistake at work. We take way too long to respond to a friend in need. We watch TV after a hard day instead of cleaning the kitchen.

We can feel like we're failing all the time. We wonder why God would call us at all.

Who are you? people ask of us.

Who am I? we ask of ourselves.

But God, the Great I AM, knows us. Knows us better than we know ourselves. We are who God designed us to be. We are glorious. We are wonderful. We are made in God's image, and we are gifts to the world.

GOD HAS PLANS FOR YOU. BIG PLANS.

I don't care if you're a CEO or a janitor, a high school student or a housewife. God has plans for you. Big plans. He loves you. He cherishes you. And right now—even as you're reading this book—He's pressing His fingers on your life, imprinting you with His holy design.

Listening for the Audible

We all can get audibles from God. I've already told you about a couple of mine. I'm sure you could tell me about yours.

Some are more philosophical. God calls me to think about something from a different angle or consider a point of view I hadn't seen before. He just wants to shift my worldview or perspective—evolve and grow. *Hey, Travis*, He'll say to me. *Let Me help you see broader. Deeper. Wider.*

But sometimes the audibles I've received have been pretty obvious. And some have changed my entire life.

We've talked about how I went to college at Georgia Southern University. When I first arrived, I didn't know how to read music. I could play several instruments, but I played mostly by ear. Whatever formal education I'd received on the piano or playing in the high school band didn't do me much good in college. A sheet of music might as well have been written in Sanskrit, as far as it would help me.

But I still loved music. While I planned to get a master's in business, I did hope to minor in music. And because I could play piano pretty well, I was certainly going to take some piano courses.

At Georgia Southern, you had to qualify for the program. And to qualify, you had to audition. And that audition required you to, in my case, play piano from a sheet of music. Right there, I was in trouble.

However, even though I was required to read music, I knew beforehand the piece I was required to play. So . . . I cheated. A music major friend of mine helped me memorize the piece. I didn't think it was any big deal. I *knew* music, even if I didn't know how to *read* music. I'd play for the professor—Natalia da Roza was her name— and she'd be impressed by my ability. She wouldn't even notice that I couldn't read the music, I told myself. And even if she *did* notice, she wouldn't care.

But unfortunately, she did notice. And she did care.

After I finished the piece, she looked at me. "You can't read this," she said, in a thick German accent.

"I can read it a little," I said.

She stared at me a little longer, and I could almost see the anger welling up in her face.

"You're trying to get educated in music without reading," she said. "That's like going to school for Spanish without speaking the language." She was furious.

Then Professor da Roza announced she was going to talk with the dean about me and stormed out of the room. She left me sitting there for what felt like thirty minutes. Honestly, I thought I had blown it. I felt a little like Moses on the run. My chances of getting a music minor looked pretty slim right then. They probably weren't even going to let me in the program.

Finally she came back, shaking her head. "I don't know why I'm doing this," she said, "but we're going to give you a shot. *One shot*. But I'm telling you," she added, her face getting tight and stern, "I'm going to be on your neck. I'm going to be on you all the time. And if you mess up, you're out of my program."

It was the beginning of a great friendship.

Professor da Roza grew to love me. She treated me like family. She taught me how to read music, and I played and played and played—honing my skills and slowly becoming a truly well-rounded pianist.

So fast-forward to my senior year. I was still on my own plan. Music's fine, but it's no way to make a living. I was planning on being a businessman.

But one day Professor da Roza asked me to sit down and talk with her.

"What are you doing after graduation?" she asked in that now-familiar accent of hers.

I didn't need to think about my answer. I *knew* what I was going to do. I had my game plan in place. "I'm going to graduate with my business degree and then get an MBA. And then I'll go to New York. Work in corporate America. Make a lot of money."

Then she asked me a question that would change my life forever: "What would you do for free?"

I didn't have to think about that either. "Music and ministry," I said.

She smiled. "Then you need to do *that* with your life."

The professor wasn't done with me yet, though. "For the rest of the semester, we're not going to work on music," she said. "I want us to map out what you want your future to be."

"Mapping out" meant printing out online images and creating a dream wall or vision board. She encouraged me to think big and provide as much detail as possible, including things like venues, tour buses, and studios.

That was it. The audible. Everything suddenly made so much sense.

Sure, it was scary. Audibles often are. It's never comfortable to move away from that plan you'd so painstakingly put together. And while I've always had a lot of confidence that God would guide my every step, I know it's not easy for everyone. While I still graduated with that business degree in 2006, I knew that wasn't my future. It was music. It was ministry. I was going to sing and play and preach for God. I knew that's what He wanted me to do. I *knew* it.

The next eight years were hard. Those were my struggle years, my digging years, my wilderness years. But even in the middle of those incredibly tough times, I never had a doubt that God had put me on the path that He wanted me to be on. The audible, delivered through my piano professor, was unmistakable.

The audible. It rocks our worlds. It changes our lives. It takes us places we'd never get to—never even think about going to—on our own.

Moses followed God's audible, and it led him back to Pharaoh's throne room where he told the king, "Let my people go!"

Fishermen, tax collectors, and others followed an audible and followed Christ—all the way to Calvary and beyond.

God's audible has taken me around the world, singing and playing in front of millions of people, where I hopefully help them see the beauty, majesty, and love of God.

The audible has called countless people, changing their lives, leading them in directions they never thought they'd go. People have dropped everything to follow God's call. They've given away fortunes and they've found them. They've taken insane chances and lived in total confidence. They've followed that audible to the ends of the earth, just like C.T. Studd did.

C.T.'s life went in a completely different direction before he died in 1931. During his last days, he said that "my only joys . . . are that when God has given me a work to do, I have not refused it." He heard an audible and followed it, just like every one of us should. He never looked back, and he never wanted to. And when C.T. died, the last word reportedly on his lips was what it will be for all who follow God's audibles—follow them without hesitation, follow them with joy and confidence.

"Hallelujah."[7]

CHAPTER TEN

Waiting for God

This book began with me talking about Forward City's miracle building—how God taught me to maximize what I had while waiting for that miracle to be fulfilled; how God answered our prayers and somehow pulled the finances together to buy an old Best Buy; how God brought the right resources together to turn that Best Buy into a big, beautiful church. When we pray for the right things— for our prayers to align with what God wants from us, to follow His instruction, to maximize everything that He's already given us— amazing things can happen. Forward City is proof. Miracles can multiply.

God's been so good to us. So generous. And because He answered Forward City's prayers in such a staggering way, I find myself starting the process all over again.

As I write these words, Forward City is the fastest-growing church in South Carolina. Over one hundred adults join each *month*, bringing their kids with them and inviting their friends. In the first nine months of 2023, about a thousand people were saved, and we've been discipling them—walking alongside them as they make a real commitment to Christ. We've baptized hundreds of folks. We've reached thousands of kids.

And you know where that leaves us? Right where we started. We've outgrown our building. We're straining at our seams. We're back at chapter 1. Here we *grow* again.

But it feels different this time. Yes, we're looking for property. We're exercising that faith muscle all over again. But instead of stressing about it—instead of asking God why He's not sending me everything I need for that new space *right now*—we're wrapping our arms around the process. We're praying constantly. We're maximizing the resources we have. We're keeping our eyes focused on Jesus throughout it all. We're excited about where we are. We're excited about what God's going to do.

And we're waiting.

Waiting.

But we're not standing still.

When we pray, we move our feet.

The Waiting Game

Sometimes it can feel like God is taking forever to answer our prayers. Even when we're praying for the right thing, even when we're following God as faithfully as we can, God's timeline isn't ours. And that can be incredibly frustrating.

Our calendars are full. Our time is short. And honestly, we're a little spoiled. Back in biblical days, things took *time*. It was no problem to measure the days with a sundial, because no one was in a big hurry. But today our technology allows us to maximize time like never before. We can microwave a full dinner in a couple of minutes. We can measure our days in microseconds. We get frustrated if there's a few-second lag on our web browsers. We feel the clocks in our own lives tick down our moments. God may be eternal, but we humans—at least in this life—are on the clock. And we want our blessings *now*.

Why does God make us wait?

In some ways, that's what a lot of this book has been about.

While we're waiting, God's working. He's working on our hearts, on our minds, on our maturity, on our circumstances. If God plopped a million dollars in my lap when I first asked for it, I wouldn't have used it well or wisely. It would've been a miracle wasted. When we looked at Moses in the last chapter, we saw how God used that time of waiting to develop all the necessary skills he needed—to not just lead God's chosen people, like an Egyptian ruler, but to lead them safely through the wilderness, like a shepherd.

"Patience is the companion of wisdom," the great theologian Augustine wrote.[1] I think I'd go even further. Patience helps *create* wisdom.

Think of it like a tree. Oak trees don't grow in a hurry, and you don't want them to. You don't want them to grow too tall too fast, because they won't have the root structure to sustain that growth. They wouldn't get enough water or enough nutrients. And if the roots don't go deep enough, why, the tree might just blow over with the first strong wind.

For me, that's what wisdom is: that root structure. That's what we need to sustain our spiritual growth. That's what we require to bear God's fruit—to fulfill whatever mission we might be praying for. We need those roots. We need that wisdom. And the only way to get them is through patience. We let our roots grow, getting stronger day by day, year by year.

I think that's why it took such a long time for my musical career to take off. All that time in Georgia and North Carolina, I was working on my music and producing albums. *The More*, which I released in 2007, didn't do much. *Stretching Out* in 2010 got a little more attention, but not enough to feel like I was on my way to the gospel music heights. It wasn't until I released *Intentional* in 2015 that I felt like my branches spread. That I was producing the fruit that God had planned for me.

When people ask me why it took so long for my career to take off, I tell them something I heard my friend Mike Todd say once that "big planes need long runways." I'm joking, but there's truth in that. And there's another truth too. I needed my roots to grow. I'm so grateful, looking back, that God had me wait for my success, that He made me wait for that answer to prayer. I needed to be renewed enough, transformed enough, to be able to carry the weight of whatever God wanted me to do. I didn't want to appear to be fruitful and not be rooted.

We need to wait. God knows it. And maybe in our quieter times we do too. I think most of us understand that a lot of our hurry-up culture isn't all that satisfying in the end, because anything worth doing takes time. You don't cook a real Thanksgiving dinner in the microwave. You don't write a book in a day. You don't raise kids in a month, or a year, or a decade. The time you take shows your love.

I'm forty years old now. And when I preach, I squeeze my forty years into forty minutes. I'm armed with my experience and whatever wisdom I've gathered along the way and put it right on stage. When I talk, or when I write a new song, everything I've learned goes into what I say or sing.

When you use your own wisdom, that's what you do too. When you stand up in front of a classroom or a boardroom, or when you hunker down with your kids to tell them a bedtime story or talk over dessert, you bring everything you've learned into those conversations—not what you learned in the classroom but what you've learned every day of your life. The lessons you've taken from that life. The ditches you've dug. The seasons that you've endured.

The time I've spent waiting? It's time well spent. Because that time allowed me to grow in wisdom.

But it can be hard to approach every situation with patience. Sometimes it doesn't feel like we're learning anything—it seems as if we're wasting our time. The waiting feels more mysterious—and much more frustrating.

A guy named Abraham can relate.

Packing Up, Following God

Abraham was born long before David or Moses or even Joseph. He and his family lived in the city of Ur, located in what is now southern Iraq. Back then he was called Abram, and his wife's name was Sarai.

They might've lived there for the rest of their lives. But God called an audible.

"Hey, Abram!" God said. "Go from your country and head west, to a new land I want to show you. And I'll make you a great nation, and I'll bless you and make your name great" (paraphrase of Genesis 12:1–2).

People lived longer back in Abram's day, but man, the guy was *seventy-five*—a little old, even back then, to be setting out on a wild new adventure. But he and Sarai, along with his nephew Lot, took off and headed to the land of Canaan. Once they got there, the Lord talked to Abram again, and we see what God said in Genesis 12:7: "To your offspring I will give this land" (NIV).

Great, right? I can almost hear Abram now. "Sarai, you hear that?! God's going to make my name great! He's going to give this whole country to our offspring!"

But there was a problem. Abram and Sarai didn't have any kids. Not a one. Year after year passed. Abram and Sarai were getting older and older. And by chapter 15 of Genesis, Abram was wondering whether he might've misheard God. He wondered whether his heir wasn't going to be a child of his but a *servant* of his. If he and Sarai died, his attendants would inherit everything they owned. Why not God's promises too?

God said (and I'm paraphrasing here), *No, Abram, you absolutely did not get it wrong. Look toward heaven and count the stars, if you can. So shall your offspring be.*

Abram believed God. The Bible says so, and adds that his belief was "counted as righteousness" (Genesis 15:6). Abram trusted God. He trusted Him completely.

But more time came and went, and still no kids. The years went by. And the doubt crept in.

Finally, Sarai wasn't having any more of it. She believed *part* of God's promise, but she didn't trust Him to keep it *completely*. So she told Abram to sleep with Hagar, one of her servants. Sarai was tired of waiting. Sarai was going to take matters into her own hands, presuming to know that what God said wasn't what He really meant.

That happens to us sometimes, too, doesn't it? We pray. And we wait. We pray some more. We wait some more. And finally we think that God's taking too long. We think the "not yet" is a no.

Still, God blessed Hagar with a baby. The child was called Ishmael, and he, too, became the originator of a huge number of people.

But Ishmael wasn't the child that God told Abraham to expect.

In fact, it took another thirteen years before God once again told Abram to prep himself to have a kid. Abram—now called Abraham—literally laughed at the thought. He was ninety-nine years old by that time. Sarai (now Sarah) was ninety, *way* past menopause. And when Abraham told his wife what God had told him, she laughed too. In Genesis 18:12 Sarah essentially told Abraham, "Now that I'm worn out and you're old, we're going to have a *kid*?" But God said, "Is anything too hard for the LORD?" (18:14).

Miracles are easy for God. We know that. We've *seen* that. I've felt those miracles move in my own life. Maybe you have in yours too. But sometimes we still doubt, especially if we've waited for God for a long time.

But God never backs out of a promise. He told Abraham and Sarah that they would give birth not just to a child but to a nation—a nation so big that it'd be hopeless to count its people. And the baby that would begin it all wouldn't be a metaphorical baby, or one birthed by another mother. It'd be their own birth child—one conceived in their own tent and formed in Sarah's own womb. The hurdles in the way were nothing to God. *Nothing* is too hard for the Lord.

> MIRACLES ARE EASY FOR GOD. BUT SOMETIMES WE STILL DOUBT, ESPECIALLY IF WE'VE WAITED FOR GOD FOR A LONG TIME.

What are you waiting on God for? What has He promised you?

If your desires are God's desires, you won't wait forever. If you're following God's mission, His storehouses stand ready. If you're praying for the right things—to fulfill *His* purposes, not yours—He'll honor those prayers. And if God really made you a promise, you can bank on it.

God's promises can be counted on. But we must do our part.

And the first part of our part? We need to trust. We need to walk in faith.

Thousands of years after Abraham lived, the author of Hebrews could see the promise to Abraham fulfilled. "By faith Abraham obeyed when he was called out to go to a place that he was to receive as an inheritance. And he went out, not knowing where he was going," he wrote. "By faith Sarah herself received power to conceive, even when she was past the age, since she considered him faithful who had promised. Therefore from one man, and him as good as dead, were born descendants as many as the stars of heaven and as many as the innumerable grains of sand by the seashore" (Hebrews 11:8, 11–12 ESV).

Faith. We can't lose faith when we're waiting. We can't lose faith when we're frustrated. We can't lose faith even when it seems like the promises of God are impossible.

But how do we keep that faith? How do we follow God's instruction while we live in a season of waiting?

In some ways, it's no different from the path we need to follow all the time. We need to live lives of faithfulness. Pray. Worship. Obey God's rules and guidelines for us.

And that includes one really important rule—one that, more than any others, we're likely to break. It's the one that reminds us of the importance of waiting. The importance of slowing down our crazy pace. The importance of *rest*.

I'm talking about keeping the Sabbath.

Sunday Service

Slow down, God tells us. *Slow. Down.*

We've talked about the Sabbath briefly, but I want to go back to it here, because in the context of waiting on God, it's so important. And let's be honest: it's something we don't do very well. *I* haven't always done it well.

I work on the traditional Sabbath day, like most pastors. In fact, it's the busiest day of the week for me—the day the rest of the week leads to. I'm on stage on Sundays, preaching and singing and leading prayer. And for a long time, I went straight from that working Sabbath to the regular work week. I'd show up in the Forward City offices on Monday morning, trying to concentrate on the crazy week ahead and get ready for the next Sunday.

I felt like I needed to do that—needed to squeeze every second out of the week. When we first started our church we had so much to do, so many boxes to check off. I was preaching at two services every

Sunday, and sometimes three. I had a staff to manage and care for, a church to help run. Every day required fifty decisions from me, and those decisions didn't take a day off. How could I? I didn't have *time* for a day of rest, I told myself. Not right now.

But here's the funny thing about that: When I was working seven days a week, I wasn't working as well. When I refused to turn off my engine, the gears started grinding. I wasn't as sharp or as efficient as I needed to be or as I could be. In trying to use all my time, I ended up wasting more of it.

Finally I was like, *Dude, you're tired. You're going crazy. Sit down a bit. You'll be better on Tuesday.*

And you know what? I was. Ever since I started to force myself to take a Sabbath (and trust me, sometimes it *can* feel like you're forcing yourself to take time off), I've been better for it. I feel both sharper and calmer. I don't feel like my mind is all over the place. And that in turn filters into every facet of my life. When I'm relaxed, I feel like I'm a better husband, a better father, a better leader, a better friend. I'm better when I'm rested. We all are better with rest.

Think about those Ten Commandments Moses brought down from Mount Sinai. God told us not to kill, not to commit adultery, not to steal, not to covet. These are all laws that have found their way into our secular laws today. We're told to have no other gods before God, never make idols, to remember that the Lord's name is sacred. We look at those rules, and we say, *Hey, that's good advice. That's important stuff.* We calibrate our lives to those laws. Or if we don't, most of us realize that we should.

But then, in the middle of all these unquestionably, undeniably valuable rules, we see "Remember the Sabbath and keep it holy," and we figure that *that's* the law we can do without. The other nine, fine. But the Sabbath? *No need to bother with that one,* we say.

But we have it all wrong. That commandment is just as important as all the rest. In fact, if I remember correctly, that specific commandment has more words supporting it than any other commandment. It's a big deal to God. In the same space that God talks about murder and adultery, He says, *Hey, by the way, take a day of rest.*

Yes, Jesus did say that the Sabbath was made for man, not man for the Sabbath. But Jesus also talked often about its importance. He never suggested getting rid of it. Why is it such a big deal? Well, for one, and as I wrote earlier, God knows that we need the rest. He knows how distracted we can get, how frazzled our lives can be. In that space of Sabbath we can find new focus. We can reset, recreate, recalibrate, realign.

Taking the Sabbath also reminds us of the value—the beauty, really—of our seasons of waiting. We force ourselves to slow down. We *wait* to take care of all the stuff on our to-do lists, all the work calling for our attention at the office, all the time-eating beasts we have to feed. We remember that we're not slaves to time; we're servants of God. He calls the shots, not our phones or calendars. We wait. And when we wait, we're able to engage so much better with the tasks we've been given.

Likewise, because God sometimes withholds our blessings for a time and forces us to wait for them, we're given the space to know, mentally and emotionally, how to use them. We plan for them better. And, I might add, we're in a position to enjoy those blessings more. Think about Abraham and Sarah. They would've loved Isaac, their only son together, had he come around when they were twenty years old, I'm sure. But the fact that they had to wait for him? I bet they treasured him even more—and were more able to see Isaac for the miracle that he was.

But the importance of the Sabbath goes even beyond that. To take a Sabbath is an act of trust. It's a demonstration of faith.

God rested on the seventh day, but God didn't need to. No, He was, in the very beginning, giving us an example of how *we* should be living. And it's a critical part of how we should relate to God.

Let me explain that. God knows just as well as we do how busy we are. But when we take that day off, we're saying to God that we're turning our lives and our schedules over to Him. We're trusting that God knows better than we do how to manage our time. We're trusting that, by sacrificing time—our most precious resource we have in this life—that sacrifice will not only bring glory to God but benefit us too.

"Hey, I'd rather trust You with six days than trust myself with seven," we're telling God. It's the same concept as the tithe (the biblical directive of giving 10 percent of our income to church). We're saying, "I trust you with 90 percent more than I trust myself with 100 percent."

We sometimes pray for the wrong thing. We pray for more time to do the things we want or need, when we should be praying to manage wisely the time or resources we have. And the wisest thing we can do with a day of our time is to give it to God—who turns around and gives it back to us to rest and recharge. We find that we get more done in those six days than we would in seven—and our minds and hearts are more centered, more focused, more open to God.

Every time we sacrifice something for God, we're telling Him, "I trust You." That's what sacrifice is. When Gideon built an altar and sacrificed his oxen, you don't think he could've used that meat for himself? With those Midianites running rampant over the promised land, food was in short supply. A cynic might've said, "Hey, kill that steer, but eat the meat yourself; you'll need your strength." But no, Gideon gave it to God and said, "I trust You."

Trust and faith are all about sowing those seeds in our lives. When we hold on to what we have in clenched fists—be it money or time—we're admitting to ourselves that that's all it'll ever be. If we have a dollar in our fist and keep it there, it'll just be a dollar. And believe it or not, it works the same with time. If we grasp a minute in our hand, it'll vanish in sixty seconds.

But when we sow—when we turn our resources over to God, and

that includes our time—we're trusting God that what we hold can be more, with His help and His guidance. We sow our seeds and expect a harvest. We plant our resources and *wait* for them to grow.

That sense of sowing is harder to see when we're planting *time*. We know that time isn't like grain. Your time doesn't multiply like corn. You don't plant one seed of time and, after a few months, see a dozen stalks grow. We think that time doesn't work that way. And for us, it doesn't. But for a God who lives outside of time? An eternal, infinite God who'll be here long after this universe itself spins to a halt? God has, literally, all the time in the world. And when we sacrifice some of our precious time at His altar, He can multiply it. Because we're rested, we work better. Because we're at peace, we play better. We become less the frantic shells of ourselves resulting from too much work and too little rest, and we grow more into the men and women God designed us to be.

TAKING A SABBATH DOESN'T END OUR WAITING, BUT IT CAN HELP REDUCE OUR WORRYING.

Taking a Sabbath doesn't end our waiting, but it can help reduce our worrying. We think more clearly, and that helps us to see God more clearly. When we rest, we trust.

And when we trust, we rest. That doesn't mean we don't have work to do. That doesn't mean that we stay still. But when we say, "God, I know You've got this under control," it allows us to relax. We move not in fear but in confidence. It's like in basketball, when you're dribbling the ball up the court and you know where your teammates are—and who might be open to take a shot.

Working While You Wait

"How long, O Lord?"

That's how Psalm 13 begins. We're told that it's a psalm of David, a man after God's own heart. This isn't the only time David seemed frustrated by God taking way too much time to fulfill prayers. In the first two verses David continued: "Will You forget me forever? How long will You hide Your face from me? How long shall I take counsel in my soul, having sorrow in my heart daily? How long will my enemy be exalted over me?"

David did a lot of waiting in his long and varied life, and, I'm sure, so have you.

But he didn't stay still. Even as he waited, David worked. And so should we.

The prophet Samuel anointed David as the next king of Israel when David was just a kid, tending his father's sheep. It was about fifteen years before he actually became king. But in between, he killed a giant, played music in the palace, led Israel's armies, fled the country in fear of his life, pretended he was crazy, worked with Israel's arch-enemies the Philistines, and fought in a bloody civil war.

David was waiting. And he was *working*. This shepherd who was anointed king spent a lot of time doing exactly what we've been talking about throughout this book: He maximized his resources. He managed his people. He followed God's instructions and demonstrated incredible faith.

That doesn't mean that David didn't make mistakes. He made plenty of them. But for the most part, he followed the Lord with both zeal and wisdom. He took an active role in the miracles God gave him; he understood that the Lord sometimes granted joint custody in His miracles.

For me, the word "patience" is synonymous with another: "preparation." God never meant for us to sit on our hands. You won't find that in Scripture. To wait on the Lord means you're *waiting on the Lord*— that is, you're acting as a waiter in a restaurant. A *servant*, in other words. You're serving the Lord Almighty, and you're still participating in His work—whatever He has asked you to do.

It encourages me to see that even David—a man after God's own heart—sometimes felt the anguish of waiting. But with the king's psalms, it never ends with waiting. It ends with trusting.

And so, even though Psalm 13 begins with complaining—"How long, O LORD?"—it doesn't end there. Instead, it concludes with this: "But I have trusted in your steadfast love; my heart shall rejoice in your salvation. I will sing to the LORD, because he has dealt bountifully with me" (verses 5–6 ESV).

Trust. Faith. It can be hard to lean into either when we're waiting for God to answer our prayers. But it's so critical. *So* critical.

Which of your prayers are waiting on God?

How has waiting for answered prayers helped your wisdom to grow? Your roots to deepen?

How are you spending your time waiting? Are you standing still? Or are you still working?

Do you conscientiously take a Sabbath? Do you allow yourself to rest?

CHAPTER ELEVEN

Amen

In his book *Prayer: Does It Make Any Difference?* Philip Yancey asks a provocative question: "Does prayer change God or change me?"

If you could sum up this book in seven words, those come close.

So often in our lives, we pray for the wrong things. We only pray for Him to give us a miracle or shower us with blessings or just give us the stuff that we think we need. We pray for resources and wealth and happiness. We pray for God to act the way *we want Him to.* And when He doesn't conform to our wishes right away, or when He fails to meet our own little timeline, we think that God's letting us down.

Sometimes that comes dangerously close to asking God to change. We're asking God to change His posture toward a given problem, His attitude toward something that's stressing us out. We're always asking. But sometimes, when we pray, we don't listen for how God's answering.

If we listened, we might hear God whisper back, *If I gave you what you want, what would you do with it? If I gave you resources, how would you spend them? If I gave you healing, how would you use it? If I gave you peace, would you really be at peace? Would you receive peace and appreciate it? Or would you just find something new to be anxious about?*

There's nothing wrong with asking God for what you want or what you need. The Bible *encourages* us to ask:

- "Be anxious for nothing, but in everything by prayer and supplication, with thanksgiving, let your requests be made known to God." (Philippians 4:6)
- "The prayer of a righteous person has great power as it is working." (James 5:16 ESV)
- "Therefore I tell you, whatever you ask in prayer, believe that you have received it, and it will be yours." (Mark 11:24 ESV)

Prayer—consistent prayer, persistent prayer—even becomes the subject for one of Jesus' most famous parables, and one that I think shows Jesus' sense of humor too.

Jesus told the story in Luke 18:1–8. He introduced His disciples to a judge who, we're told in the New King James Version, "did not fear God nor regard man." He sounded like a bit of a jerk.

But Jesus said that a widow lived in the same town. She had apparently been wronged by someone, and she wanted justice. So she went up to the judge and asked him to do something about it.

At first, the judge did nothing. But the widow kept pestering him. And finally, just to get some peace and quiet, the judge decided to help. "Though I neither fear God nor respect man, yet because this widow keeps bothering me, I will give her justice, so that she will not beat me down by her continual coming" (Luke 18:4–5 ESV).

Jesus told the disciples that, if a mean old judge finally did the right thing because this widow kept asking him to, how much more thoroughly, and more beautifully, will an all-loving God answer our righteous prayers? The answer might not be immediate. We're all familiar with the "not yet" answer. But will the answer come? You bet, Jesus tells us.

The entire parable was introduced by Luke as a story about prayer—how the disciples, and we, should "always . . . pray and not lose heart" (18:1 ESV).

Jesus makes it clear: Pray for what you want. Pray for what you need. Pray, because God answers. God cares. God gives.

It's not wrong to pray for a miracle. It's not wrong to pray for money, health, relationships. It's not wrong to, as the widow in Jesus' story does, pray for justice. God can, and He does, answer those prayers *if* they're compatible with His plans. And if you don't steward that answered prayer properly, even *answered* prayers can get messy.

> **PRAY FOR YOUR MIRACLES. BUT IN THE MIDST OF YOUR PRAYERS, THINK ABOUT YOUR ROLE IN THEM.**

Yes, pray for your miracles. But in the midst of your prayers, think about your role in them. Ask about your involvement. Examine yourself to determine if you're ready.

Praying to change God is a nonstarter. Pray to change yourself.

Be the Change

Change isn't easy. Ask me. Ask Forward City Church.

I was so happy when we bought that building, that old Best Buy, for cash. It was truly a miracle—a miracle that our congregation had joint custody of.

But really, the work was just beginning. You can't just move a church into a Best Buy. That doesn't work. The roof and the outside walls were there. But everything else? We needed to change it.

So I printed out the plans of the building—a massive sheet of white paper as big as a kitchen table. Maybe bigger. I'd take that plan with me everywhere—that and a red pen. I even took it to bed.

I—along with Matt Edwards, a Forward City executive pastor in charge of operations and strategy—started dreaming about what we really needed to do to make our building a usable, functional, beautiful church. We talked about moving walls. *This space needs to be bigger,* I'd say. *We need to move that room over here. We need to have a massive space dedicated to children.* And then, as the process went along, we took the next step: we literally started taping imaginary walls on the carpet. We drew every single room in tape.

But I didn't know how to build the actual rooms. I've never built anything in my *life.* I've hardly even fixed anything. I've never even changed the oil in my car. Change a 44,000-square-foot building? That's a big ask. I was guessing.

I didn't know anything about city sewage requirements. I didn't know what a conduit was. I didn't know anything about drywall. And even studying the plans, even eyeballing the tape, I didn't really know how big the rooms would actually be—or how big we needed them to be. When construction started, the carpenters would be framing walls, and I'd come in and look. "No, no," I'd say. "That's going to be too small." So they'd have to rip down what they'd done and start over.

They called them "change orders." I was changing everything. We spent a significant amount of money on change orders. Turns out, not only is change hard, but it's also pricey.

Thankfully I got a little help. We brought in a guy named David Fink, who worked for a Tulsa, Oklahoma, architectural company called Churches by Daniels. He moved here for a year and oversaw everything—the entire construction process. David took a huge weight off my back, and for a solid year he was my best friend.

We'd talk every day. I'd ask a ton of questions: "Why do we have to do that?" "What are all those cords over there?" "What are you doing that for?" Every day I peppered him with those questions. David must've gotten tired of answering them, but he never showed it. And over time I learned. I knew why we needed to do certain things and how to do them.

Thanks to that year, I've become a little bit of a construction master. I can tell you everything you'd ever want to know about conduit. And David? Well, he and his wife, Pam—"Mama," we call her—have made Forward City their home church. Wherever they are in the country, we can count on them checking in with us, praying for us, and worshipping with us online just about every other week.

In a way, our building experience mirrors a little of what God is doing with us through the process of prayer—and He's doing it sometimes with our interference, sometimes with our help. We make our own plans. We mark the walls of our own lives. And God loves to see those plans. "If you abide in Me, and My words abide in you, you will ask what you desire, and it shall be done for you," Jesus told us in John 15:7.

But that word "abide" is so key here. If you're building your hopes on a shaky foundation—in other words, a foundation that's not Him—God can't help you. But as we talk to God—as we pray—as we discern His plans and align with His will for us, our plans and His get closer and closer together. His wishes become our wishes. And over time, we build something beautiful.

Trust and Faith

Probably my favorite verse in all of Scripture is Romans 8:28: "And we know that all things work together for good to those who love God, to those who are the called according to His purpose."

I believe that—believe it with all my heart. I believe it so much that sometimes people think I live in a fantasy world. I believe that things will *absolutely* work out. I believe in the goodness of people.

I'm like, "Hey, everybody loves everybody!" And some of those people caution that I should pump the brakes a little.

"Travis," they'll tell me, "life is not like this. People are out there who'll try to take advantage of you."

"No way!" I'll tell them. "Everybody has integrity!"

Truth is, sometimes those people in my life are right. Not everyone's good. Not everyone has integrity. But I'm wired to trust. I'm wired to see God's grace in everything I do, every aspect of my life. I've seen too much, and overcome too much, to doubt. In my life, all things have worked together for good. It might not have always worked the way I thought it would, or on the timeline I would've liked. But all things *have* worked together. God has blessed me through my successes. He has loved me through my failures. He has taught me to dig in during the hard times. And when I look forward, I know God will have plenty more blessings for me, plenty more hardships to endure, plenty more audibles to follow.

But the most important part of that verse for me isn't the "all things work together for good" part—the part that most people gravitate toward and hang up on their refrigerators. It's the "to those who love God, to those who are the called according to His purpose" part.

That verse echoes what I believe prayer is about.

Prayer isn't a one-way suggestion box. When we pray, we have a conversation with God. We approach the throne of the Holiest of Holies and—get this—can talk with Him. Not just to Him; *with* Him. And that means that God speaks back. That's the "those who love God" part, because we listen to those we love. That's the "called according to His purpose" part, because just as we ask things of God, God asks things of us. He asks us to use His gifts well and wisely. He calls audibles.

And the more we talk with God, the more we're changed. The more our hearts align with His.

As mentioned before in one of my favorite verses, Romans 12:2, "And do not be conformed to this world, but be transformed by the renewing of your mind, that you may prove what is that good and acceptable and perfect will of God."

Do not be conformed to this world, the verse says. How often do our prayers conform not to God but to this world? How often does the world tell us what we should ask for? What we should value? When we ask God for something, are we asking for His permission to value something outside His will? Are we asking for *confirmation* for our *conformation*?

No, we're supposed to be *transformed*—changed through the renewing of our minds. And prayer is absolutely critical if we truly want to be transformed. When we speak to God sincerely, and when we listen to Him, how can we *not* be transformed? How can we *not* be changed?

For me, renewal is revelation. My mind is renewed by the wisdom I receive. That's not solely through prayer. It can come through my studying Scripture. It can be through the voice of my pastor and mentor, Matthew K. Thompson. It can come through late-night talks with my love, Jackie. It can be through my friends—the Bible says that "iron sharpens iron." But much of it comes through the Holy Spirit in prayer. The Holy Spirit teaches and leads and corrects in prayer—and through all of that it transforms me. Sometimes it's a nudge, but more often for me, it's a full-blown new way of looking at things, a sudden deeper understanding. Once the truth is revealed to me, my mind starts turning differently. I'm changed. That moment in the SUV was a transformational moment. That conversation I had with Professor da Roza was a transformational moment. Those were pivot points in my life—times when I was going one way and, with God's grace, I turned around and went the *right* way.

It reminds me of that old hymn "What a Friend We Have in

Jesus." The hymn is all about the power of prayer—the blessing it is to take all of our hopes and fears and concerns and ambitions to God and hand them over to Him.

> O what peace we often forfeit
> O what needless pain we bear,
> All because we do not carry
> Everything to God in prayer.[1]

When I stay in my own head and focus on just my own thoughts and feelings, there's no possibility of revelation. It's only by conversing with someone else—really talking and really listening—that I give myself an opportunity to change. I need people in my life that not only confirm me but challenge me. My wife, my kids, my pastor, my mom, my friends. And most especially, I need God. Through prayer, I receive His instruction and revelation. Through prayer, I hear my audibles. Through prayer, I transform.

I can either hold on to frustration or lay it on the Author of all things and get a greater revelation. I carry everything to God in prayer.

The Best Example

When we bring everything to God in prayer, we sometimes pray for the wrong thing. And you know what? That's okay. It's not like God gets mad. He knows our wants and needs and limitations. He understands our suffering. God, through Jesus, was one of us once, after all. He knows what it's like to be hungry or thirsty or tired. He knows what it's like to not have enough (because He got an earful on that from His own disciples). He even knows what it's like to *pray* . . . and not get the answer He wanted.

But you know what else Jesus did? He showed us how to pray for the right thing.

PRAY FOR THE RIGHT PEOPLE. We all know that Jesus was accompanied by people as He traveled and preached, and central to His ministry were His twelve disciples. But what did Jesus do before He gathered them to His side? He *prayed*. "Now it came to pass in those days that He went out to the mountain to pray, and continued all night in prayer to God" (Luke 6:12). In the very next verse we're told that "He called His disciples to Himself."

Look at their resumes. Most didn't have the skills you'd think Jesus would need. There wasn't a prophet in the crew. Not a single religious scholar. Most were blue-collar folks who'd spent their days working with their hands. It wasn't the sort of team we would've picked if we'd had the entire human race to choose from. Not only did they not (at least on the surface) have the right skill sets but they also didn't have the raw numbers they needed. When you think about what Jesus was trying to do—save the entire world—twelve people seems like a pretty small staff. But Jesus knew what He was doing. He understood the process He wanted to employ. He knew how to maximize the skills and talents of those who followed Him.

We don't all lead people, but we all know people. We all count on people. We all need people. We can pray to God that we find the right ones to help us through the tough spots in our lives—and just as important, pray that we can be the right people in the lives of others.

But it's good to remember another thing about those disciples too. Every single one of them let Jesus down. They fell asleep in the garden of Gethsemane when Jesus was in His most agonizing hours. They denied Him during the long night before His crucifixion. And one outright betrayed him. A man that Jesus had chosen after hours and hours of prayer.

Yet all of them had a place in God's plan. And most of them

went on to do some incredible works after Jesus was gone, spreading the good news throughout the known world. Even when they disappointed Jesus and walked away, Christ had work in store for them: hard work and blessings too. Are you okay with God using people who used you? God Himself was.

MAXIMIZE WHAT'S LEFT. When Jesus was preaching to a crowd of five thousand people, His disciples worried about how they were going to feed them all. One kid in the crowd apparently had five loaves of barley bread and two small fish, but that was it. "What are they among so many?" Andrew asked Jesus.

What did Jesus do? He asked His disciples to make the people sit down. He took the loaves and the fish. And then He prayed—not for a miracle but with thanksgiving for what they had in hand. "And Jesus took the loaves, and when He had *given thanks* He distributed them to the disciples, and the disciples to those sitting down; and likewise of the fish, as much as they wanted" (John 6:11).

The story echoes Elisha and the woman with the jar of oil, doesn't it? Jesus could've just miraculously made food appear, but He didn't. He accepted a gift of bread and fish—giving the boy who gave it participation in the miracle. Jesus took what was left. He maximized what He had, and in His hands it was multiplied. Exponentially multiplied.

FOCUS ON FAITHFULNESS, NOT FAVOR. Jesus didn't want to be crucified. When Christ and His disciples made their way into the garden of Gethsemane, Jesus was "troubled and deeply distressed. . . . 'My soul is exceedingly sorrowful, even to death'" (Mark 14:33–34). He was so anxious, so worried, that he started sweating "great drops of blood falling down to the ground" (Luke 22:44).

Jesus knew what was in store for Him. He knew what He had to do. But Jesus was human too. He didn't want to do it. And when He prayed—a prayer recorded in the three synoptic Gospels—Christ asked His Father for a favor.

"Father, if it is Your will, take this cup away from Me," Jesus prayed. "Nevertheless, not My will, but Yours, be done" (Luke 22:42).

Yours be done. When we're aligned with God, all our prayers ultimately come to those three words. When we're transformed by God, we learn to trust in Him. We learn to follow—even when part of us might want to run the other way. We follow in faith, wherever God leads.

FORGIVE. At the very end of His life—even as He was crucified—Jesus prayed one of the most startling prayers in all of Scripture. "Father, forgive them, for they do not know what they do" (Luke 23:34).

Forgiveness can be the most challenging part of our journey. I know it is for me. Maybe it's the most challenging part of all our journeys. The wounds we suffer at the hands of others go deep. But God sometimes speaks to me in metaphors, and one day He told me this: *Your heart is a house.*

What does that mean? It's just this: Every home, whether it's a mansion or a shack, has limitations. It has only so many bedrooms, so many bathrooms, so many cupboards to fit your stuff. If your heart is a house, it only has so much room in it.

When you don't forgive someone, that bitterness and anger and the mere presence of that person take up space in your heart. They take up a room. They can even take up a whole wing. And when those rooms in your heart are gone, they're gone. When we let those old hurts and betrayals get to us, it's like that person is still there in our lives, even if they're long gone. It's almost as if they're holding that room hostage—not letting anything or anyone else in.

But while it can feel like a hostage situation, guess what? We still have the key. We can unlock that door. Sometimes we need to let people go. Sometimes we need to let go of all the anger and hostility surrounding those people. Sometimes we need to clean out those rooms to make space for something, or somebody, else—somebody who can make our house better and brighter and more life-giving.

Jesus was the perfect person, and He modeled prayer perfectly. He prayed before big decisions (Luke 6:12–13). He prayed before miracles (John 6:11), and after them (Luke 5:16), and sometimes even while doing them (Mark 7:31–37). He prayed alone (Mark 1:35–36) and with people (Matthew 26:26). And He prayed—just like we do—for blessings for Himself, His friends, and for us all (John 17:1–26).

But mostly, He prayed to do God's will.

It's right there in Matthew 6:10—right near the top of the prayer Jesus taught us all to pray.

That prayer—the Lord's Prayer as we know it today—says it all, really. In five verses, Jesus showed us what prayer should look like—how to pray for the right thing. From Matthew 6:9–13:

> Our Father in heaven,
> Hallowed be Your name.
> *(Keep your eyes focused on God.)*
> Your kingdom come.
> Your will be done
> On earth as it is in heaven.
> *(Pray to fulfill His wishes—not for Him to fulfill your own.)*
> Give us this day our daily bread.
> And forgive us our debts,
> As we forgive our debtors.
> *(Ask for what you need. Ask for grace. And ask God to*
>   *give you grace too—to be okay with God using the*
>   *people who used you.)*
> And do not lead us into temptation,
> But deliver us from the evil one.
> *(Pray to draw nearer to Him every day, every week, every year.)*
> For Yours is the kingdom and the power and the glory
>   forever. Amen.

What are you praying for? Are you praying to change God? Or are you praying for God to change you?

Pray.

Pray for your heart's desires, pray for healing, pray for God to work miracles in your life. But pray as well for God to maximize what you have in your life now. Pray to move joyfully into the future, not to grumble about the past. And pray, always, that your desires will be God's desires. That your will is His will.

> **PRAY, ALWAYS, THAT YOUR DESIRES WILL BE GOD'S DESIRES. THAT YOUR WILL IS HIS WILL.**

Pray to be a blessing. Pray to be a gift. And if you do, God's own blessings and gifts will come.

Amen.

Certain words feel powerful, don't they? And one of those words is "amen."

We end every prayer with that word. It doesn't matter what we're praying for or when or where or for how long. "Amen" is the period at the end of the prayer. We say it so often that we can lose sight of what it really means. *True.*

Okay, so it means slightly more than that. It can be interpreted as "so be it" or "certainly" or "verily." Its meaning can take on slightly different shades depending on how it's used. A shout of "amen!" during a sermon doesn't mean *quite* the same thing as when you're in somber prayer. But that core sense of truth is a part of "amen" however you use it, and its essential meaning has been the same in the thousands of years we've used it. It means that what has been said is true. Who we're directing the prayer to is the source of truth. And what we've asked for *in* that prayer, we believe faithfully that it *will* come true.

In prayer, that word "amen" is a statement of faith. It's a seal on our communication with God. We're saying that we *believe.* We believe in the One we're talking to. We believe in His ability to see it come to pass. We say the word in confidence—that in directing our pleas to the One who can heal every wound and dry every tear, we're putting our wants and needs, our anxieties and our hopes, in good hands. The best, most reliable hands imaginable.

But when we pray our prayers and say our amens, God says something to us too.

What will you do with what I give you?

God can change our circumstances. He can change our health, address, lifestyles, relationships, jobs. But God, first and foremost, wants to change *us*. He can change our hearts and our desires. And honestly? As we change, we can change the world. We ask for healing, but we can also heal. We ask for gifts, but we can give. We ask for help, but we can be the helpers. The quickest way to a miracle is to become one. Be what you need.

God wants to bless us. But He wants us to bless others too. He wants us to sow so that we can reap. He wants us to spread His love—like grain, like oil, like loaves and fishes.

When I pray, I pray for change—change not just in my circumstances but my life. I pray for wisdom and growth. I pray that when I'm blessed, I might bless others. I pray that when I'm in a valley, I can dig ditches. I pray that when I sing and preach, the people listening to me might—as they sing and dance and pray themselves—feel God standing with them. Standing with His arms open and a smile on His face. I pray that when I do my thing, God's doing *His* thing—and He's working through me.

My prayer for you is that God will work through you too. That you'll pray not just for miracles but for management. Not just for stuff but for strategy. Pray not just for God's gifts but that God turns you into a living gift for others—blessed beyond measure and blessing the people around you in turn. And I pray that as you begin to pray for the right thing, that God will do His thing in your life.

Amen.

Acknowledgments

To my dear **JACKIE:** You inspire me more than anyone. I'm grateful and honored to do life with you. Thank you for birthing and raising three kings: Jace, Josh, and Judah. You carry so much responsibility, yet you do it with so much grace. Thank you for believing in this project. Your support is primary.

To my mom and hero **CHARLEATHER**, aka Mama Greene: All that I am is because of all that you've done. With the option of quitting on life after the sudden death of my dad, you refused to. You trained my sisters, Kim and Londa, and myself in how to live holy, eliminating any excuse we could ever make to rebel against God.

To my pastor and mentor **MATTHEW THOMPSON:** I have no idea how I ever existed without you in my life. You have coached, counseled, and championed me to reach new heights, both naturally and spiritually. Every human needs a pastor like you. Thank you for being a spiritual covering for both my wife and me.

To my friend and collaborator **PAUL ASAY:** You are truly a genius. Working on this with you was challenging and fun. Thank you for pushing me beyond my limitations and provoking thoughts that I believe will help so many people. I told you this multiple times, but I'll say it again: I don't want to do another book without you. Your approach to writing and thinking is second to none.

To my brother and inspiration, **MICHAEL TODD**: You have helped me in ways that deserve much more than a paragraph. You are the most selfless influencer I've ever met. You love genuinely, you give extravagantly, you share wisdom and opportunities. More important, you actually care and want others to win. Thank you for being you and for seeing us.

To the super-team of ladies who made this book happen: **JANET TALBERT, LISA JACKSON,** and **DENISE BROWN**. Thank you for believing before anyone else did. Before I typed and spoke a single word, you cheered for me. You never once doubted the success of this work. You deserve all the roses that could possibly be collected. I am forever indebted to each of you.

To the men who taught me how to be a man: Your example made me a better leader, thinker, husband, and father. Thank you **UNCLE JOHNNY HEMINGWAY, JERMONE GLENN, JOHN GRAY, STEVEN FURTICK, DAVID CLARKE, PAUL ADEFARASIN, JOEL OSTEEN, TUDOR BISMARK, SHOMARI WHITE,** and **DAVID CHADWICK**. Your constant accessibility and advice has shifted the trajectory of my life.

The final individual I have to show love to is **MATTHEW EDWARDS**. You are a true brother, friend, co-laborer, and a bona fide winner. Jordan had Pippin; I got Matt! Every pastor needs a Matt. It would take an additional book to write about how much value you add to my vision and to my life. Thank you for staring at nothing with me and continuing to dream.

Finally, to **FORWARD CITY CHURCH** and every Forward Citizen around the globe: Leading you is one of the top joys of my life. You continue to take a chance on a color-haired, sneaker-wearing, radical visionary. Your passion is incomparable. From the staff to every dream-team member, you are the standard. The lessons captured in this book were taught to me by you. Even if I wasn't your pastor, there's no other church I would want to be connected to.

Notes

Chapter 1: Are You Ready for What You're Praying For?

1. "Mo Money Mo Problems," featuring Mase and Diddy, The Notorious B.I.G., track 10 on *Life After Death*, Bad Boy Records and Arista Records, 1997.

Chapter 2: Catching the Rhythm of Spiritual Discipline

1. Angela Morrow, "How Long Can You Go Without Food?," Verywell Health, updated April 22, 2023, https://www.verywellhealth.com /how-long-live-without-food-1132033.
2. "How George Müller Started His Day," GeorgeMuller.org, December 20, 2019, https://www.georgemuller.org/devotional/how-george-muller -started-his-day4006229.

Chapter 3: Making God's Dreams Yours

1. Stew Smith, "Military Boot Camp at a Glance," Military.com, May 8, 2012, https://www.military.com/join-armed-forces/military-basic -training-boot-camp.html.

Chapter 4: Shift the Focus from Stuff to Strategy

1. Advait Jajodia, "'I Wanted to Be the Best Basketball Player to Ever Play': When Kobe Bryant Revealed the Deal with Himself at 13-Years -Old That Helped Him Become One of the Greatest Ever," The SportsRush, May 6, 2022, https://thesportsrush.com/nba-news-i-wanted

-to-be-the-best-basketball-player-to-ever-play-when-kobe-bryant-revealed
-the-deal-with-himself-at-13-years-old-that-helped-him-become-one-of
-the-greatest-ever.

2. John Celestand, "Why Kobe Bryant Inspires Me," *Our Brave New World* (blog), March 18, 2008, http://awbutler.blogspot.com/2008/03/why-kobe-bryant-inspires-me.html.

3. David, "Storytime: Team USA Trainer Tells a Story About Kobe's Insane Work Ethic," Ballislife, March 6, 2014, https://ballislife.com/storytime-team-usa-trainer-kobe.

Chapter 6: Pray for the *Right* People

1. Editors of the Encyclopaedia Britannica, "Midianite: Ancient People," Britannica, October 26, 2023, https://www.britannica.com/topic/Midianites.

2. Erin Urban, "What Is Your Impact?," *Forbes*, October 16, 2017, https://www.forbes.com/sites/forbescoachescouncil/2017/10/16/what-is-your-impact.

Chapter 7: How to Pray When You're Expecting a Miracle

1. Kyle Davison Bair, "Can We Ever Prove Mathematically That Our Universe Was Designed by God?," Medium, January 25, 2021, https://medium.com/hope-youre-curious/can-we-ever-prove-mathematically-that-our-universe-was-designed-by-god-e8f0bb885285.

2. "Made a Way," track 5 on Travis Greene, *The Hill*, RCA Records, 2015, https://www.youtube.com/watch?v=MimVg0OMGvA.

Chapter 8: Concentrate on What's Left—Not Who Left

1. David G. Allan, "Let Us Now Praise Single Moms," CNN Health, August 8, 2023, https://www.cnn.com/2023/05/14/health/single-mom-parenting-wellness/index.html.

2. Jennifer Vanderminden et al., "Rates of Neglect in a National Sample: Child and Family Characteristics and Psychological Impact," *Child Abuse & Neglect* 88 (February 2019): 256–65, https://doi.org/10.1016/j.chiabu.2018.11.014.

Chapter 9: When God Calls an Audible

1. Martin Williamson, "A Short History of the Ashes," ESPN, September 19, 2006, https://espncricinfo.com/story/a-short-history-of-the-ashes-259985.

2. "C.T. Studd," Men Who Saw Revival, accessed November 15, 2023, http://menwhosawrevival.blogspot.com/p/ct-studd.html.

3. "£25,000 in 1860 Is Worth £3,748, 588.83 Today," CPI Inflation Calculator, accessed November 15, 2023, https://www.officialdata.org/1860-GBP-in-2018?amount=25000.

4. Stephen Ross, "Charles Thomas (C.T.) Studd," Wholesome Words, accessed November 15, 2023, https://www.wholesomewords.org/missions/biostudd.html.

5. "C.T. Studd," Men Who Saw Revival.

6. "Spread of Christianity," WorldData.info, accessed November 15, 2023, https://www.worlddata.info/religions/christianity.php.

7. Claude Hickman, "History of Mission: C.T. Studd," The Traveling Team, accessed November 15, 2023, https://www.thetravelingteam.org/articles/ct-studd.

Chapter 10: Waiting for God

1. Saint Augustine, from *Nicene and Post-Nicene Fathers, First Series*, vol. 3, ed. Philip Schaff, trans. H. Browne (Buffalo, NY: Christian Literature Publishing Co., 1887), quoted and edited by Kevin Knight, "On Patience," New Advent, accessed November 15, 2023, https://www.newadvent.org/fathers/1315.htm.

Chapter 11: Amen

1. Joseph Medlicott Scriven, "What a Friend We Have in Jesus (1855)," Hymnary, accessed November 16, 2023, https://hymnary.org/text/what_a_friend_we_have_in_jesus_all_our_s.

About the Author

Travis Greene is the lead pastor of one of the country's most vibrant and impactful churches, Forward City (Columbia, SC). He is passionate about helping the unchurched and overchurched move forward with God. In addition to touring as an award-winning singer, he speaks as a leading voice for this generation at several prominent churches including Transformation Church, Elevation Church, Lakewood Church, ONE LA, and Social Dallas. Travis married the love of his life, Jackie, in 2011, and together they have three energetic boys: Jace, Josh, and Judah.

CONNECT WITH TRAVIS

Website: travisgreene.tv

Social Media: @travisgreenetv

NOTES

NOTES

NOTES

_____

_____

_____

_____

_____

_____

_____

_____

_____

_____

_____

_____

_____

NOTES

NOTES

NOTES

NOTES

_____

_____

_____

_____

_____

_____

_____

_____

_____

_____

_____

_____

_____

NOTES

NOTES